Bead Creative Art Quilts

Chase your dreams!

Nancy Eha

Bead Creative Art Quilts

Nancy Eha

 Creative Visions Press

 Creative Visions Press
4890 Neal Avenue North
Stillwater, MN 55082
www.beadcreative.com

Book design and composition:
  Amy Kirkpatrick, Kirkpatrick Design
  Dorie McClelland, Spring Book Design
Photography: Jim Altobell, Altobell Imagery
Test beader: Brita Hedblom
Cover art quilt and beading: Nancy Eha
Title page art quilt: Sharon Commins, USA, beading: Nancy Eha
Contents page art quilt and beading: Nancy Eha

Library of Congress Cataloging-in-Publication Data
Library of Congress Control Number: 2005910917

Eha, Nancy
Bead Creative Art Quilts

ISBN 13: 978-0-9656476-3-2
ISBN 10: 0-9656476-3-3
Printed in the United States of America
06 07 08 09 10   5 4 3 2 1

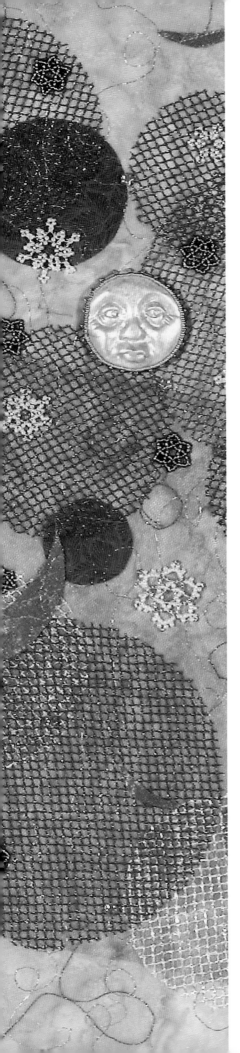

Contents

Page 1   Challenge the Myth and Create Magic!

Page 3   Golden Rules for Beading on Fabric

Page 5   Fabric, Beads & Tools

Page 11   Beaded Art Garments

Page 15   Beading Secrets Revealed

Page 19   Basic Bead Embroidery & Beyond

Page 27   Beaded Coils

Page 31   Writing with Beads

Page 35   Elevated Beading

Page 39   Setting a Cabochon with Beads

Page 43   Beaded Kaleidoscopes

Page 53   Large Beaded Images

Page 57   Beaded Dragonfly

Page 67   Beaded Snowflakes & Stars

Page 71   Constructing a Beaded Art Quilt

Page 79   Creating Paper Stitch Patterns

Page 80   Grids for Bead Designs

Page 90   Patterns for Large Beaded Images

Page 92   Illustrations for Left-Handed Beaders

Page 95   Glossary

"I think that if one kind of property is sacred,

it's the kind that is the product of our own minds,

made with our own hands . . ."

Camille Pissarro
French painter, 1830–1903

Challenge the Myth and Create Magic!

Challenge the myth that beads add only sparkle to art quilts and instead create beaded magic!

Visualize art quilts from a new perspective, one in which beads are not added for mere sparkle, but applied as a primary design element.

This book will be your guide as you uncover new and dynamic beading techniques that go far beyond traditional fabric beading stitches. Two chapters will answer technical questions about the use of beading supplies and art quilt construction: Fabric, Beads, & Tools, and Constructing a Beaded Art Quilt. Practice the beading stitches in Basic Bead Embroidery & Beyond; these stitches are the foundation for the innovative beading techniques included in this book. And if you want to spend more time beading and less time taking out "mistakes," be sure to read Golden Rules for Beading on Fabric and Beading Secrets Revealed.

This book would not be possible without the collaboration of the international fabric artists whose amazing art quilts grace the pages of this book and serve as the foundation for my beading. Not knowing what beading techniques I would add to their quilts, these artists exercised a huge leap of faith by sharing with me their personal visions of art quilts. Supplied with only a desirable finished quilt size, a vague color range to work within, and a request from me to "do what you do best," I was overwhelmed with their talent and creativity as each quilt was delivered to my doorstep. To them, this book is dedicated:

Linda Colsh, Everberg, Belgium

Sharon Commins, Los Angeles, California, USA

Sophie Gelfi, La Bourboule, France

Rayna Gillman, West Orange, New Jersey, USA

Heidi Lund, Bremerton, Washington, USA

Amira Wishinsky, Tel-Aviv, Israel

Happy Beading!
Nancy Eha

Art quilt by Linda Colsh, Belgium
Beading by Nancy Eha

Golden Rules for Beading on Fabric

Want to spend more time beading and less time trying to "fix" what has been done?

The following information is worth reviewing as you begin each new fabric beading project. Page numbers are listed after each entry, directing you to a section in the book for a more detailed explanation. These are the "Ah-Ha's!" and the "I wish I would have known that sooner!" that I have compiled via my own beading "learning experiences."

The criteria for choosing which tips would make the list of Golden Rules was simple. Several students in my workshops must have exclaimed, "That information alone was worth the price of admission!"

Purchase beads and supplies from a source that specializes in beading supplies.
See page 6, **Bead Sources.**

Test beads for colorfastness if the beadwork will be washed or dry-cleaned.
See page 6, **Testing Beads for Color Permanence.**

How to decide what bead colors to use.
See pages 5–6, **Color Considerations.**

Match the thread color to the bead color, not the fabric color.
See page 9, **Thread Color.**

Always bead with the thread doubled.
See page 9, first column color bar.

Never remove beads or stitches by back tracking with the needle point first.
See page 17, **Milking the Cow.**

If the thread stitch on the wrong side of the fabric will be more than 1 inch long, knot and cut off the thread before moving the needle to a new location.
See page 17, **To Knot or Not to Knot.**

If thread stitches on the back of a project are undesirable, do not bead as the final step of construction.
See page 71, **Beading the Quilt Top.**

Fabric, Beads & Tools

Starting with properly prepared fabric and appropriate supplies will make your time beading more pleasurable and provide you with a quality outcome.

Fabric

Pre-wash and iron all fabric for a beading project that will be washed or dry cleaned in the future. All weights of fabric may be beaded, but consider your personal preferences and use of your finished project when choosing the fabric.

Stabilizing Fabric

Upholstery and other heavyweight fabrics are sturdy enough to support the weight of the beads without a fabric stabilizer. Woven fusible interfacing is necessary for sheer and lightweight fabrics such as silk, for which the grain of fabric can shift. Woven fusible interfacing is found on bolts in most fabric stores. This interfacing is available in several weights, featherweight or lightweight being the best for lightweight fabrics. Following the manufacturer's instructions, fuse the woven fusible interfacing with an iron onto the wrong side of the fabric before cutting fabric pieces for use in a project. Stabilize lightweight fabrics prior to piecing, even if using a fabric foundation such as muslin for crazy quilts.

Caution: the use of non-woven fusible interfacing may leave a dot pattern on the right side of lightweight fabrics. Once folded, fabric with non-woven fusible interfacing will retain a permanent crease. Always use woven fusible interfacing.

Fabric Prints as Inspiration

A printed commercial fabric may be an inspirational starting point for beading. The color and design of the fabric print may be used as a guide for placement of bead color, bead texture, or bead stitch direction. A printed fabric pattern may also serve as an inspiration for coordinating additional fabric and bead colors. Look at the fabric print and then acquire other fabrics and beads for your project that are color matches, saturated or less saturated versions of the colors, or tints and shades of the colors on the fabric print.

Color Considerations

Bead Color Applied to Fabric Color

Beads are tiny pixels of color and light, far smaller than fabric pieces. For the eye to see color contrast at this extremely small scale, it is necessary to have greater color contrast between beads and fabric than what would be needed between two small pieces of fabric.

Use beads of high color contrast to the background fabric color if the beads are a primary design element. Opaque beads achieve the greatest color contrast on a fabric background. Transparent or translucent beads will allow both the thread color and the fabric color to filter through the bead color.

If the beadwork is intended to represent texture and not be a high contrast to the fabric, choose a bead similar in color and value to that of the background fabric. Or, pair clear glass beads with the fabric; the color of the fabric will show through the beads. Clear beads also provide the design option of changing the appearance of the bead color each time you change the beading thread color.

Color Principles for Beading on Fabric

Use these color principles to your advantage when combining bead and fabric colors.

1. Warm colors always appear to move to the foreground and cool colors retreat to the background.

2. Saturated colors always appear to move to the foreground and less saturated colors retreat to the background.

3. Three-dimensional beads attached to two-dimensional fabric give the illusion of the beads moving to the foreground independent of whether the beads are warm or cool colors, or are saturated or less saturated in color than the fabric. This is an important consideration when designing an art quilt landscape or seascape.

To increase the illusion of depth in a landscape or seascape, place beading in the foreground, or place larger beads in the foreground and smaller beads in the background nearer the horizon.

Beads

Testing Beads for Color Permanence

An increasing number of dyed seed bead and bugle bead colors are entering the marketplace. Beads are not porous to accept dye as fibers can; the bead "dyeing" process is, in fact, a surface application of color. Certain colors cannot be made in glass production. Instead, an application of color is added to the bead surface. Beads that are probably dyed are blue-purple, magenta, and some reds.

Determining whether a bead has an added surface color is important because not all surface applications will remain on the bead when it comes in contact with water or body oils. The possibility of the color washing or rubbing off has no correlation to the purchase price of the beads. Galvanized beads may also lose their color due to moisture or body oils.

If you plan to wash or dry-clean a beaded project in the future, test all bead colors before you start your beading project. Put water and a few drops of dish washing detergent in a small bowl. Take a pinch of beads from each color of beads you will use in the project and add the beads to the bowl. Wait two or more hours,

remove the beads from the bowl, and dry the beads. Do not use any beads that have changed or lost color. Or, sew a few beads from each color of beads to the inner hem of a garment and have the garment dry-cleaned.

Be sure to buy enough beads for your project. The bead color may change with each new batch or dye lot.

Bead Sources

I highly recommend that you shop at a local bead store, an internet bead source, or a vendor at a show whose primary products are beads and beading supplies. This will assure a high quality purchase at a fair price. Avoid sources that sell a vast array of craft supplies and large "bargain" bags of beads. Although prices may seem low, most low priced "bargain" bags contain misshapen beads that are grossly inconsistent in size, which will provide undesirable results. To find a bead store in your area, look up BEADS in your telephone directory.

Seed Beads

Seed beads are categorized by size, color, and country of origin. Seed beads, also known by the French term rocailles, are small elliptical glass beads that are cut from long tubes of glass and tumbled in hot sand to round the edges and polish the glass. Seed bead sizes are numbered according to diameter—the larger the number, the smaller the seed bead. Sizes available for purchase from bead retailers range from a small size 15° to a large size 6°. Size 11° beads, the size most commonly used for beading, are readily available. Prior to World War II, tiny size 18° to size 24° beads were manufactured in Europe. These vintage beads occasionally can be purchased from antique dealers. The smaller the bead you select for your project, the finer detail you can achieve.

> Look closely at several colors of seed beads that are sold as the same size. Bead sizes can be inconsistent, both within the same color of a size of beads and also between colors of the same size.

Country of Origin

The majority of seed beads are imported into the United States from two countries: Japan and the Czech Republic. Japanese seed beads and bugle beads are imported in half-kilo bags containing beads that are all the same color and size. Retail shops repackage Japanese beads into plastic tubes or small bags for resale. Czech seed beads and bugle beads are imported on hanks. The number of strands on the hanks may vary. Hanks look like pre-strung necklaces and are frequently displayed on peg boards in retail shops.

Both Japan and the Czech Republic produce a vast array of bead colors and applied bead finishes. Japanese seed beads are more consistent in size and have larger holes. Larger holes are preferable for most beading stitches as the needle and thread may pass through the same small seed bead hole several times. If the hole becomes clogged with thread and you try to force the needle through, the needle will break or the bead will shatter.

Seed Bead Shape and Color

Illustration 1

Shape

Look closely at a number of different colors of seed beads. Note that the shape may vary from an elliptical shape to a barrel shape *(Illustration 1)*. Barrel shaped means the bead is not rounded off around the hole as is an elliptical bead. Silver-lined and matte beads are usually barrel shaped. A magnifying glass may be useful in identifying the difference in shape. The shape of the bead is significant when constructing a sharply curved line of beads; elliptical beads will create a smoother curve.

Color

By pairing glass colors with surface finish applications, thousands of seed bead colors are possible. After an opaque or transparent glass bead

is manufactured, surface finishes may be applied over the glass. Surface finishes include: **A** luster (shiny), **B** matte or frosted (produced by etching glass), **C** matte iridescent (iridescent applied to matte), **D** iris (multicolored metallic iridescent), **E** matte luster (satin pearly), **F** Ceylon (pearly luminescence), **G** galvanized (opaque metallic), and **H** AB or burora borealis (pastel iridescent). If a surface finish is added inside the bead's hole, it is called a lined bead. The hole finishes most commonly applied are **I** silver-lined (reflective silver finish) or **J** color-lined (a dye color in the hole that contrasts to the glass bead color). It is visually exciting to use a variety of bead color and surface applications together in a project.

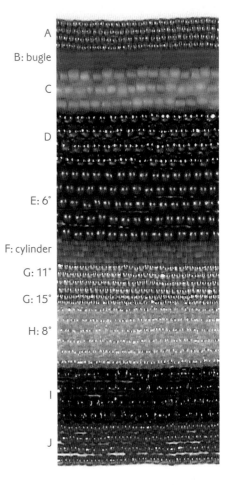

A
B: bugle
C
D
E: 6°
F: cylinder
G: 11°
G: 15°
H: 8°
I
J

Sunlight will cause bead colors to fade. Never store or display beads in direct sunlight, even for short periods of time.

Cylinder Beads

Cylinder beads are produced in Japan and are sold under various names, depending on the manufacturer. They are short tubular beads that are very uniform in size and have large holes. Cylinder beads are an excellent choice for a bead loom or needlewoven beadwork when tight fitting beads are needed to form charted patterns. Because of their shape, cylinder beads may not produce smooth results when constructing sharply curved beaded lines on fabric.

Bugle Beads

Manufactured in a manner similar to seed beads, bugle beads are cut into short tubes from a longer glass tube. The diameter of most bugle beads is usually the same as an 11° seed bead; the length can range from ⅛" to 2". Bugle beads are usually not tumbled in hot sand; therefore, the edge around the hole can be sharp and sometimes jagged.

Japanese bugle bead ends are smoother than Czech bugle beads. If the bugle bead edge is jagged, use an emery board to file it flat. The fabric of a garment may shift and move during wear, and the jagged edge of a bugle bead can cut through the beading thread. Bugle beads attached to wearables should be bracketed with a seed bead on each side. Bracketing a bugle bead with seed beads will prevent the beading thread from being cut by the bugle bead edge as the fabric shifts. Or, FireLine may be substituted as beading thread. Bracketing bugle beads with seed beads or using FireLine is not necessary for an art quilt that will hang on a wall.

Accent Beads

A bead is anything with a hole through it! Any object that has a hole through it, or that you make a hole through, can become a bead.

Accent beads include glass, plastic, bone, shell, pearl, and metal beads. A large variety of accent beads are available at most full-line bead stores. You may also find discarded accent beads at yard sales. With the exception of faux pearls and metal beads, soiled beads may be soaked in soapy water and/or brushed clean with an old toothbrush. Most metal beads and buttons will eventually tarnish and corrode. Over time, corroding metal against the fabric may soil and rot the fabric.

Thread

Thread Strength

A strong thread is needed to hold beads securely to fabric. Nylon beading thread is stronger than natural or synthetic sewing thread. Monofilament thread is not a good choice. It is difficult to maintain secure knots with this type of thread.

Silamide is my thread choice for most beading projects. This nylon thread, which looks like a cotton/polyester thread, is available at some bead retail stores. Sold on 40-yard cards and 600-yard spools, 20+ colors are available, only in size A. Silamide's twisted fibers are lightly pre-waxed, which helps prevent tangling and twisting. Historically used by tailors to attach buttons to high-end clothing, Silamide was adopted by beaders in the 1990s.

Crystals, metal beads, and the jagged edges on some bugle beads can cut through Silamide thread. For these beads, FireLine, a braided bead thread and fishing line, is stronger and a better choice. Purchase the smoke color 4-lb Test/Size B weight FireLine for fabric beading. FireLine can be threaded

into a size 12 Sharps or size 12 long beading needle. Do not use your best embroidery scissors to cut Fire-Line, it will quickly dull the blades on the scissors.

> Double thread will keep the beadwork secure if one thread should break. Double thread also provides the opportunity to remove stitches or beads without having to remove the needle from the thread. See Milking the Cow, page 17.

Thread Color

How do you determine the best color of beading thread for a beading project? Answer: choose a thread color the same color or nearly the same color as the beads. Or, choose a neutral thread color that is the same value as the bead color. For example: off-white or a cream color thread for light value pastel beads, a gray thread for medium value beads, and dark blue for most dark value beads. Small amounts of thread will be visible with some beading stitches. The thread will be less noticeable when the thread color matches the beads, not the fabric. Knot on the wrong side of the fabric and change thread color as needed, or pre-thread several needles with different colors of thread.

Needles

Beading needles have a size numbering system, as do seed beads. The larger the needle number, the thinner the needle. Some sources recommend purchasing a needle size corresponding to the bead size. As beads are numbered by the outside diameter not the hole size, this rule of thumb may not be accurate.

Use a size 12 Sharps or size 12 long beading needle for seed bead sizes 15°, 14°, 11°, 10°, 8° and 6°. When passing the needle through a 15° or 14° seed bead more than once, a single, not double, thread may be an option. Or, for beads smaller than 11°, use a size 13 Sharps needle or size 13 long beading needle.

Sharps needles are about 1" long. Long beading needles are about 2½" long. Long needles are more flexible and tend to break quicker. They also have smaller eyes, making threading a needle more difficult. Sharps needles may be purchased at bead stores, needlework shops, and some quilt shops. Most bead stores stock both Sharps and long needles. If you have large fingers, long beading needles will provide additional needle space for picking up beads. Some beaders find a magnifier or magnifying lamp a great help both for threading needles and beading.

Needle Threaders

When using a needle threader to thread a beading needle, pull the needle threader out of the needle eye by grasping the wire close to the eye of the needle with your fingers. Sharps and long beading needles have very small eyes and it is easy to break the wire off the threader. Purchase inexpensive needle threaders.

Scissors

A small sharp scissors such as an embroidery scissors is necessary for making clean cuts on beading thread. A small sharp pair of scissors will provide a cleaner cut than large dressmaker shears. If the thread frays with every cut or as soon as the thread touches the needle, it is usually due to the scissors. Try another pair of scissors or use a thread cutter.

A thread cutter has a small blade inserted into the holder in such a way that only extremely small areas of the blade edge are visible. To cut the thread, thread is pulled firmly over the cutting blade. A thread cutter or small blunt tipped scissors is a must for beading during air travel.

Embroidery Hoop

A hoop may be used when beading a small, isolated area of fabric. However, once an area is beaded, the beaded area will not fit between the two parts of the hoop. Using thumb tacks to tack the fabric to a wood frame is another option. With a large project, a frame becomes cumbersome, as you may not be able to reach under the frame to the area you want to bead.

To bead without a hoop or wooden frame, hand baste flannel in a 3" grid pattern to the wrong side of the quilt top fabric. Or, iron low-loft fusible batting to the wrong side of the fabric. The beading thread will pass through both layers with the thread stitches and knots remaining on the wrong side of the flannel/batting. For most beading stitches, the flannel/batting provides enough buffer for moderate thread tension and helps prevent the fabric from puckering. When the quilt back is added, the thread stitches and knots will be hidden between the wrong side of the flannel/batting and the quilt back.

An embroidery hoop or frame does help maintain proper thread tension, which eliminates most fabric puckering and distortion of the fabric. If you do use an embroidery hoop, remember to remove the fabric from the hoop after each stitching session. Leaving fabric in the hoop for periods of time will distort and stretch the fabric. Certain beading stitches require many tight thread stitches in a small area. These stitches will require the use of an embroidery hoop or frame. Technique and project instructions in this book will note if using a hoop is needed for that technique or project.

Pliers

Flat nose pliers are useful if the needle becomes stuck within a seed bead. To avoid breaking the needle, always grasp the needle with the pliers as close to the bead as possible. Grasp the needle point with the pliers where the needle exits the bead and pull the needle through. Or, grasp the needle with the pliers where the needle enters the bead and push it through. Small rubber needle grips, sold in the sewing notion area of fabric or needlework stores, are also useful. In an emergency, use a large rubber band as a needle grip.

Work Surface

Choose a white surface on which to place your beads when beading. A white surface will allow you to see the true color of the beads. Some beaders prefer a white cloth such as Ultrasuede, felt, or other low nap cloth. I prefer a small non-semented white glass or china plate. See Ergonomics, page 11. When flying, pack a white flexible plastic lid from a tub of frozen dairy topping, margarine, or large yogurt container. By squeezing opposite edges of the plastic lid together with one hand, it is easy to quickly pour the beads back into a small re-sealable zipper bag for take-off and landing.

Personal lamps that have natural or full spectrum light bulbs are best for seeing the true color of the beads.

Ergonomics

Good lighting and a comfortable chair with back support are a must for beading. To prevent back and shoulder pain, elevate the work surface to mid-chest level by placing magazines or a sturdy box under the beading cloth or plate. Slide your chair forward so that you are near the table and hold the fabric in your hands above the beading cloth or plate. In this position, you will bend from your neck, not from your back, as you pick up beads onto the needle. To avoid sore back muscles, do not hold the fabric on your lap. And do not place the work surface in a location where you must reach or twist your body to pick up the beads with the needle.

Picking up beads onto the needle out of small bead compartments causes the wrist to twist with each bead. This may cause pain in the wrist and increase the likelihood of repetitive motion problems. Avoid using a divided container or a plate with small compartments.

Make it a habit to stand up and stretch your body every half hour and to exercise your eyes by looking across the room for several minutes. If you find you lose track of time, set a timer and place it across the room. When the timer goes off, it will force you to get up and turn it off.

Beaded Art Garments

Special preparations and planning are necessary to ensure that a beaded art garment remains as spectacular as the day it was completed.

Pre-Wash Fabric

Always take the time to pre-wash the garment or fabric before beading if you plan to wash the project in the future. Many fabrics will shrink when washed for the first time. If a garment is washed for the first time after beading is completed, the fabric may shrink and pucker and the beads may lose color.

Test Beads for Color Permanence

Bead color may wear off when in contact with body oils, or come off when washed or dry-cleaned. Always test beads for color permanence before beginning to bead on a garment or accessory. See Testing for Beads for Color Permanence, page 6.

Beading by Nancy Eha

Stabilize Fabrics before Beading

Sheer and lightweight fabrics, knits, and fleece must be reinforced prior to moderate to heavy beading to avoid surface distortion caused by the beading thread tension. The following stabilizing products are available in fabric stores.

Water-soluble stabilizer is a good choice for very sheer fabrics. Baste in place to the wrong side of the fabric and remove with water once the beading is completed.

Woven fusible interfacing works well for lightweight fabrics and lightweight knits. Purchase feath-erweight or lightweight interfacing and follow the manufacturer's directions. Do not use it on an area of fabric that drapes over the body; the added stiffness of this interfacing reduces the fabric's ability to drape. Tricot fusible interfacing will allow lightweight knits to drape. Always test the interfacing product on a fabric scrap before fusing it to the fabric or garment. Caution: non-woven fusible interfacing applied to fabric will maintain a crease if the fabric is folded. Apply non-woven fusible interfacing to fabric only if the area will remain flat in storage and when worn.

Non-fusible interfacing works well for small areas on medium-weight knit garments and sweatshirt fleece. Thicker and stiffer than fusible interfacing, it is basted to the wrong side of the fabric before moderate to heavy amounts of beading are applied. After beading, remove all excess interfacing with a scissors by carefully cutting around the outer perimeter of the beading stitches on the interfacing. This stiff interfacing remains on the wrong side of the fabric behind the beading.

Prevent the Beading Thread from Breaking

Beaded art garments and accessories may rub against other objects while worn, causing the thread to break or be cut by a sharp edge on the bead. The likelihood of a bead cutting the thread increases when using beads that have sharp or jagged edges in or around the bead hole; such as bugle beads, crystals, and metal beads.

1 Bracket bugle beads, crystals, and metal beads with seed beads on either end so the edges of the bead hole do not come in contact with the thread. Or, use FireLine 4-lb. Test/Size B braided bead thread in place of Silamide thread.

2 Always bead with double thread and knot off on the wrong side of the fabric after every 3–4 thread stitches into the fabric. When using double thread, if one thread breaks, the remaining thread will hold the beading in place. If both threads break, only a few beads will come off.

3 Avoid beading techniques that include lines of beads elevated above the fabric surface. The elevated bead lines may catch on other objects and break the thread.

Before beading

After beading

Fabric print as an inspiration for beading
Beading by Nancy Eha

Beading Secrets Revealed

Review this chapter before beginning a new beading project. Not only will you achieve professional-looking results, but your time spent beading will become more enjoyable.

Mission Not Impossible: Threading the Needle

1 Start with a 2-yard length of Silamide thread; lengths longer than 2 yards encourage tangling. Cut the thread with a very sharp small scissors. The end of thread that comes off the card or spool first is usually easier to thread.

Pull the pre-waxed cut end through the thumb and index finger to flatten and press the fibers together *(Illustration 1)*. Do not attempt to moisten the waxed thread, as wax will repel moisture.

2 At a diagonal, cut the flattened end of thread with a sharp small scissors. The diagonal point will help guide the thread through the needle eye *(Illustration 2)*.

3 Hold the thread between the thumb and index finger ¼" from the cut point. Guide the thread point through the needle eye, or bring the needle eye to the thread point.

4 Needles are manufactured in such a way that one side of the eye may have a clearer passage than the other. If it is difficult to pass the thread point through one side of the needle eye, try the other side of the eye.

5 If during the threading process the thread frays, it usually indicates that the scissors used to cut the thread are not sharp enough for this application.

Illustration 1

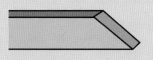

Pull through thumb and index finger to flatten fibers together.

Illustration 2

Cut thread at a diagonal with sharp scissors.

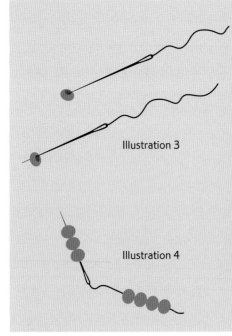

Illustration 3

Illustration 4

Magical Flying Seed Beads

1 Push down on the bead hole with the needle point; the bead will "pop" onto the needle *(Illustration 3)*. Tilt the needle point upward and grasp the bead and needle between the index finger and thumb.

2 Continue "popping" on beads and hold several beads on the needle between the index finger and thumb.

3 With several beads on the needle, tilt the needle point upward and lift the index finger off of the needle. The beads will slide down the needle and onto the thread *(Illustration 4)*. Push the beads down the thread to the fabric before beginning to bead.

Precision Beading Demystified

To achieve precise beading stitches, always pass the needle and thread through the fabric perpendicular to the fabric, never at an angle. Pull the needle and thread all the way through the fabric before taking the next thread or beading stitch.

Illustration 5

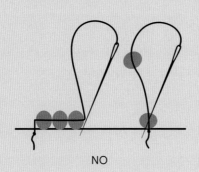

NO

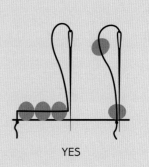

YES

Milking the Cow

Always bead with a length of double thread. If you "change your mind" about a stitch placement, double thread in the needle will make it much easier to remove beads or stitches using a technique I call "Milking the Cow."

1 Pull on the beads or thread of the last stitch you made. Pull the beads/thread stitch until the eye of the needle is snug to the fabric (*Illustration 6*).

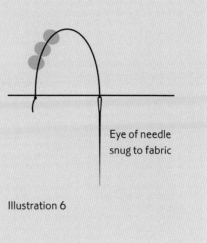

Eye of needle
snug to fabric

Illustration 6

2 If the needle cannot easily be pulled eye first through the fabric to remove the beads/thread stitch, hold the thread with both hands, one hand on either side of the fabric. Pull the thread back and forth in a sawing or "milking" motion (*Illustration 7*). This will open up the fabric fibers so the needle can pass eye first through the fabric. Never push the needle point or eye through beads or fabric; thread tangles and unwanted knots will result.

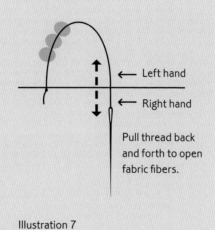

← Left hand

← Right hand

Pull thread back
and forth to open
fabric fibers.

Illustration 7

To Knot or Not to Knot

To help prevent the fabric from puckering, never make thread stitches over 1" long on the wrong side of the fabric. If a thread stitch on the wrong side of the fabric will be greater than 1" in length, knot close to the fabric, cut off the thread, knot the tails together, and resume beading in a new location.

The Disappearing Thread Act

Small amounts of thread will be visible with some beading stitches. The thread will be less noticeable if the thread color or value matches the beads, not the fabric.

Seaming-ly Easy

Keep all beading ½" in from all raw edges of the fabric if the fabric will be stitched or appliquéd to other fabric pieces, borders, or binding. The raw edges may need to be trimmed, and additional space is needed when sewing a ¼" seam due to the extra bulk created by beading. After the seams are sewn; beading can be added to unbeaded areas near the seams.

Basic Bead Embroidery & Beyond

These Bead Embroidery stitches are the foundation for the more elaborated beading techniques presented in this book. It is strongly recommended that you become familiar with both the name and construction process of these stitches before exploring additional chapters.

Supplies:

Background fabric or project on which to bead

Optional: embroidery hoop

Embroidery or other small scissors

Beads and Beading Supplies:

Assortment of beads: size 11° and 6° seed beads, bugle beads

Silamide thread: coordinate in color or value with beads

Size 12 Sharps or long beading needle

Review:

Beading Secrets Revealed, pages 15–17

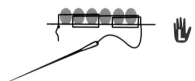

Size 11° seed beads are the most frequently used size of bead for beadwork. Explore creative possibilities by experimenting with different sizes of beads.

Illustration 1

Illustration 2

Beaded Back Stitch

The Beaded Back Stitch is a controlled, continuous line of securely attached beads on the fabric surface. A continuous secure line of beads is useful for outlining shapes, filling in an area, or writing text.

This stitch may be worked with any number of beads in an increment; a 3-bead increment is recommended (*Illustration 1*). The smaller the number of beads applied per increment, the greater the control you will have over the direction and shape of the bead line. If, when completing a line of Beaded Back Stitch, a space large enough for only 1 or 2 beads remains, add 1 or 2 beads. Step-by-step directions are on page 20.

Creating a Smooth Back Stitch

To smooth and straighten a completed line of Beaded Back Stitch, pass the needle and thread through the bead holes of the entire bead line again without stitching into the fabric (*Illustration 2*). Upon reaching the end of the bead line, pass the needle to the wrong side of the fabric and knot the thread.

Art quilt by Heidi Lund, USA
Beading by Nancy Eha

 See page 92 for the left-handed version of this illustration.

Back Stitch

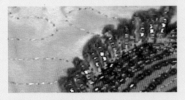

Beaded Long Stitch

Single Bead Stitch

Stop Stitch

Back Stitch: Straight Line

1 Cut a 2-yard length of Silamide thread. Thread a needle and tie the thread tails together in a knot. You now have a 1-yard length of double thread.

2 Pick up 3 beads on the needle and let the beads fall down the thread to the fabric. Lay the beads in position on the fabric without excess thread showing between the beads.

3 Pass the needle and thread through the fabric to the wrong side of the fabric at the end of the last bead, Bead 3 *(Illustration 3A)*.

Illustration 3A

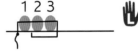

4 Pass the needle and thread through the fabric to the right side of the fabric between Bead 1 and Bead 2. Without taking another stitch into the fabric, pass the needle and thread through Bead 2 and out Bead 3.

5 The needle and thread is now exiting Bead 3.

6 Repeat #2 through #5 with the new Bead 1 touching Bead 3 of the last increment of 3 beads *(Illustration 3B)*.

Illustration 3B

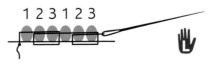

Back Stitch: Curved Line

1 For a planned curved line: draw a line or outline on tissue paper and pin in place to the fabric, or follow a line on a commercial print fabric.

2 Cut a 2-yard length of Silamide thread. Thread a needle and tie the thread tails together in a knot. You now have a 1-yard length of double thread.

3 Pick up 3 beads on the needle and let the beads fall down the thread to the fabric. Lay the beads in position on the line on the tissue paper/fabric without excess thread showing between beads.

4 Hold the beads in place on the line on the tissue paper/fabric with the thumb of your non-beading hand.

5 Pass the needle and thread through the fabric to the wrong side of the fabric at the end of the last bead, Bead 3 *(Illustration 3A)*.

6 Pass the needle and thread through the fabric to the right side of the fabric between Bead 1 and Bead 2. Without taking another stitch into the fabric, pass the needle and thread through Bead 2 and out Bead 3.

7 Repeat #3 through #6 *(Illustration 3B)*.

8 Remove tissue paper when line of beads or outline of the shape is completed.

 See page 92 for the left-handed version of this illustration.

Beaded Long Stitch

The Beaded Long Stitch is a line of beads that may be sewn to the fabric in any direction. The number of beads applied in one stitch may range from 2 to 12+ beads. The completed Beaded Long Stitch is not as secure as the Beaded Back Stitch *(Illustration 4)*. Use the Beaded Back Stitch for beading a large area or for a long, controlled, secure line of beads on the fabric.

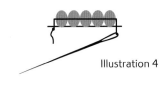

Illustration 4

1 Cut a 2-yard length of Silamide thread. Thread a needle and tie the thread tails together in a knot. You now have a 1-yard length of double thread.

2 Pick up the desired number of beads on the needle and let the beads fall down the thread to the fabric. Lay the beads on the fabric without excess thread showing between the beads.

3 Pass the needle and thread through the fabric to the wrong side of the fabric at the end of the last bead.

4 Pass the needle and thread through the fabric to the right side of the fabric in position to start the next Beaded Long Stitch.

5 Repeat #2 through #4.

Single Bead Stitch

A Single Bead Stitch is simply sewing down 1 bead onto the fabric surface. Other sources may refer to this stitch as the Seed Stitch or Running Stitch *(Illustration 7)*.

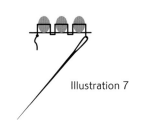

Illustration 7

Once attached to fabric, the Seed Bead hole of a Single Bead Stitch may lay vertically or horizontally depending on whether the needle and thread pass through the fabric to the wrong side next to, or under the Single Bead Stitch. If the hole is to be unseen (horizontal to fabric), lay the bead on the fabric and pass the needle and thread through the fabric to the wrong side of the fabric directly at the edge of the bead hole.

Stop Stitch

The Stop Stitch is a 2-bead stitch that stands upright on the fabric surface. A useful textural stitch, it is also great for eliminating thread from showing when attaching sequins, flower and leaf beads, etc. The top bead in the Stop Stitch (Bead 2) is called the Stop Bead. It "stops" Bead 1 from falling off the fabric *(Illustration 8)*.

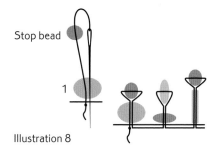

Stop bead

1

Illustration 8

1 Cut a 2-yard length of Silamide thread. Thread a needle and tie the thread tails together in a knot. You now have a 1-yard length of double thread.

2 Pick up 2 beads on the needle and let the beads fall down the thread to the fabric.

3 With only Bead 1 touching the fabric, pass the needle back through Bead 1 and through the fabric under Bead 1 to the wrong side of the fabric with one stitch.

4 Pass the needle and thread through the fabric to the right side of the fabric in position to start the next Stop Stitch.

5 Repeat #2 through #4.

Beaded Satin Stitch

Raised Satin Stitch

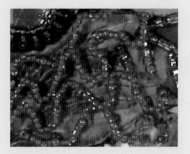

Elevated Beading

Beaded Satin Stitch

A Satin Stitch and a Long Stitch are very similar. Both are flat, straight stitches of varying lengths. A Long Stitch is called a Satin Stitch when it is used to cover or fill in an area by constructing parallel bead lines. For bead embroidery, the Beaded Back Stitch, rather than a Long or Satin Stitch, is the most secure stitch for filling in or covering an area.

Raised Satin Stitch

The Beaded Raised Satin Stitch does not lay flat on the fabric surface. Only the first and last beads of each bead line touch and connect to the fabric. This stitch can increase beaded dimension by being applied over a small raised padded form such as a piece of felt or cording (*Illustration 5*). See Beaded Coils page 27 and Beaded Dragonfly on page 57.

Illustration 5

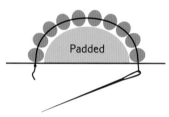

Padded

A Raised Satin Stitch may also be constructed without a padded form *(Illustration 6)*. The number of beads used in a Raised Satin Stitch without padding is limited as there is no structure in place to hold the beads up off the fabric. The following directions are for a Raised Satin Stitch without padding.

Illustration 6

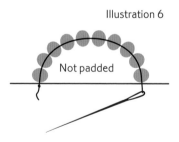

Not padded

1 Cut a 2-yard length of Silamide thread. Thread a needle and tie the thread tails together in a knot. You now have a 1-yard length of double thread.

2 Pick up the desired number of beads on the needle and let the beads fall down the thread to the fabric. Lay the beads on the fabric without excess thread showing between the beads.

3 Instead of passing the needle and thread through the fabric to the wrong side of the fabric at the end of the last bead, pass the needle and thread through the fabric to the wrong side of the fabric where the second or third to the last bead rests.

4 Pass the needle and thread through the fabric to the right side of the fabric in position to start another line of Raised Satin Stitch. You may add bead lines working in one direction (all right to left or all left to right), or alternate right to left and left to right.
The number of beads on the needle and thread is determined by the size and shape you are beading.

5 Repeat #2 through #4.

Elevated Beading

Elevated beading creates beaded texture by suspending bead lines above the fabric surface.

1 Cut a 2-yard length of Silamide thread. Thread a needle and tie the thread tails together in a knot. You now have a 1-yard length of double thread. Bead a series of Stop Stitches on the fabric.

2 With the needle and thread on the wrong side of the fabric, pass the needle and thread through the 2 beads of the last Stop Stitch constructed.

3 With the needle and thread coming out of the Stop Bead, pick up several beads on the needle and let the beads fall down the thread to the Stop Bead the thread is exiting *(Illustration 9)*.

4 Continue picking up beads with the needle until the length of the line of beads on the thread is the distance to another Stop Bead.

5 Pass the needle and thread through the Stop Bead without taking a stitch into the fabric *(Illustration 10)*. Design option: to make a curved elevated line of beads, put more beads on the needle and thread than the distance to the next Stop Bead.

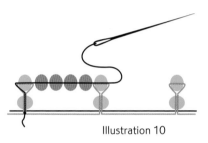

Illustration 10

6 Repeat #3 through #5. When reaching the last Stop Bead, pass the needle through the two beads of the Stop Stitch and through the fabric to the wrong side of the fabric under the Stop Stitch.

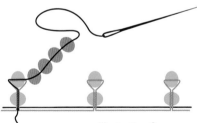

Illustration 9

Fringe

Barnacles:
A fringe variation

Bead configurations resembling barnacles can be constructed by placing a circle of Fringe on the fabric with all the bottom (Bead 1) beads touching each other. Next, pass the needle and thread through all beads of one Fringe including the Stop Bead. Connect all Stop Beads in a circle with Elevated Beading without adding beads between the Stop Beads. See Elevated Beading, page 23.

Fringe

A Fringe is a Stop Stitch that has more than two beads *(Illustration 11)*. When applied to the fabric surface, gravity will bend the Fringe downward. If applied on the fabric edge, the Fringe will hang downward.

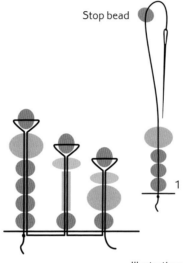

Illustration 11

1 Cut a 2-yard length of Silamide thread. Thread a needle and tie the thread tails together in a knot. You now have a 1-yard length of double thread.

2 Pick up 3 or more beads on the needle and let the beads fall down the thread to the fabric.

3 With only Bead 1 touching the fabric, pass the needle and thread back through all the beads except the last bead on the thread. The last bead is the Stop Bead.

4 When the needle reaches Bead 1, pass the needle through Bead 1 and through the fabric to the wrong side of the fabric with one stitch. If needed, adjust thread tension by holding the Stop Bead with one hand and pulling the thread as it exits the wrong side of the fabric with the other hand *(Illustration 12)*.

5 Pass the needle and thread through the fabric to the right side of the fabric in position to start the next Fringe.

6 Repeat #2 through #5.

Tightening Fringe

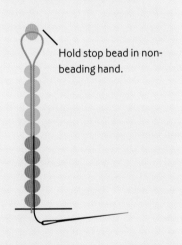

To tighten the thread tension within the Fringe: with the needle and thread on the wrong side of the fabric, hold the Stop Bead with one hand and push the other beads down the thread to the fabric. Continue holding the Stop Bead, and pull the needle and thread on the wrong side of the fabric with the other hand *(Illustration 12)*. Repeat again if necessary.

Hold stop bead in non-beading hand.

Illustration 12

Creating Long Fringe

1 If a Fringe is longer than your needle, pass the needle back toward the fabric through as many beads in a group as you can *(Illustration 13A)*. Pull the needle out of the group of beads, and then pass it through more beads. Repeat until reaching Bead 1 *(Illustration 13B)*.

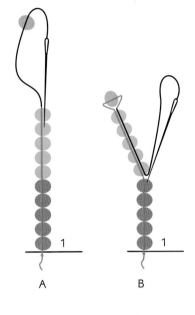

A   B

Illustration 13

2 When the needle reaches Bead 1, pass the needle through Bead 1 and through the fabric to the wrong side of the fabric with one stitch. If needed, adjust thread tension by holding the Stop Bead with one hand and pulling the thread as it exits the wrong side of the fabric with the other hand *(Illustration 12)*.

3 Pass the needle and thread through the fabric to the right side of the fabric in position to start the next Fringe.

Beaded Coils

Surprisingly easy to make, Beaded Coils are constructed by working the Beaded Raised Satin Stitch over cording that has been previously basted to fabric. Cording may be purchased in the trim or upholstery section of a fabric store; rat tail cording is found in bead stores and in some quilt shops.

Supplies:

Background fabric or project on which to bead

Embroidery hoop or needle-work frame: large enough to position the entire coil inside without repositioning the hoop

Embroidery or other small scissors

Cording with a smooth surface, any diameter. Examples: rat tail for thin coils; cotton filler cord, $^{6}/_{32}$" (4.6 mm) as photo; or thicker cording for larger coils

Straight pins

Beads and Beading Supplies:

Beads: any size or assorted sizes of seed beads

Silamide thread: coordinate in color or value with beads

Size 12 Sharps or long beading needle

Stitch:

Raised Satin Stitch

Review:

Beading Secrets Revealed, pages 15–17

Overview

Approximately three-fourths of the girth of the cording will be covered by beads. Expect the diameter of the cord to double or triple in size depending on the size of beads you use to cover the cording. As many small tight thread stitches will be made in close proximity to each other on the fabric, a hoop, frame, or fabric stretcher bars are a must to prevent the fabric from puckering.

Parallel rows of Beaded Raised Satin Stitch will be constructed over the cording. The rows of beads will enhance the roundness of the cording, not make it flat. These parallel rows must fit tightly next to each other and must stay perpendicular to the cording. You will need to adapt the direction of the beading stitches to keep the bead rows perpendicular to the cording when covering curves in the cording.

Beaded Coils are appropriate for flat fabric surfaces; they will not allow fabric to fold, pleat, or drape.

Experiment with combining different sizes of beads within a row, or position rows that are constructed with different sizes of beads next to each other.

Art quilt by Sophie Gelfi, France
Beading by Nancy Eha

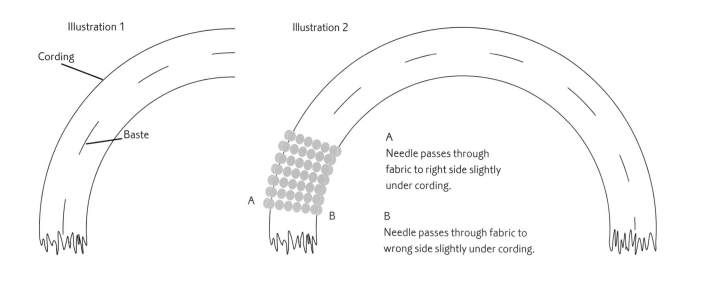

Illustration 1

Cording

Baste

Illustration 2

A

A
Needle passes through fabric to right side slightly under cording.

B

B
Needle passes through fabric to wrong side slightly under cording.

Baste Cording to Fabric

1 Insert the fabric into a hoop. Straighten the cording by running your hands down the length of it.

2 Lay the cording on the fabric. The Raised Satin Stitch will increase the girth of the cording, do not make tight angles or sharply curved shapes, nor lay parallel rows of cording close to each other. Pin the cording onto the fabric.

3 Hand baste the cording to the fabric with long running stitches. All basted stitches will be covered by beads *(Illustration 1)*.

4 If the basting stitches have flattened the cording, "plump up" the entire length of cording by squeezing the sides of the cording between your thumb and index finger.

Beading over the Cording

1 Cut a 2-yard length of Silamide thread. Thread a needle and tie the thread tails together in a knot. You now have a 1-yard length of double thread.

2 Start beading ½" or more in from the cut end of the cording. The cut edge will usually unravel; it will be easier to cover this raw edge after four or more rows of beads are added *(Illustration 2)*.

3 Pass the needle and thread to the right side of the background fabric, exiting slightly under the edge of the cording *(Illustration 2, Point A)*.

4 On the needle and thread, pick up the number of beads that will cover the girth of the cording. Wrap this row of beads over the cording to determine the correct number of beads to use.

5 After the correct number of beads are on the thread, pass the needle and thread slightly under the opposite side of the cording to the wrong side of the background fabric *(Illustration 2, Point B)*.

6 Repeat #3 through #5, covering the cord with wrapped parallel rows of beads using the Raised Satin Stitch. When you reach a curve in the cording and the parallel rows are no longer perpendicular to the cording, see Beading Curves, #7.

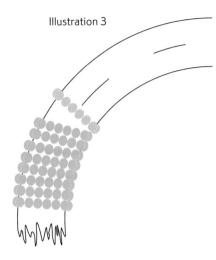

Illustration 3

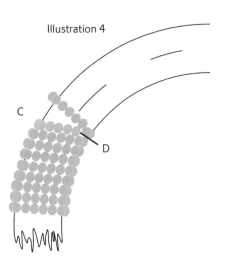

Illustration 4

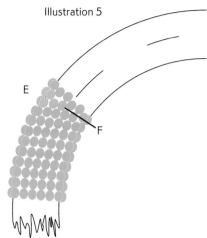

Illustration 5

Beading Curves

7 Add a row of Raised Satin Stitch from the inside of the curve near the previous row to the outside point of the curve, making this new row of beads perpendicular to the cording *(Illustration 3)*.

8 Fill in the wedge of bare cording with partial rows of Raised Satin Stitch (C, D), passing the needle and thread under the beads already in the wedge point when necessary. Then, pass the needle and thread slightly under the cording edge at the inner curve and through the fabric to the wrong side of the fabric *(Illustration 4, Points C, D)*.

9 Pass the needle and thread to the right side of the fabric, exiting slightly under the edge of the cording at the outer curve. On the needle and thread, pick up the number of beads that will cover the girth of the cording and reach to the beads already in the wedge

point *(Illustration 5, Points E, F)*. Pass the needle and thread under the beads in the wedge point and through the fabric, as if you had added a full row of Raised Satin Stitch. Repeat partial slightly-angled rows of Raised Satin Stitch until the wedge of bare cording is completely covered *(Illustration 5)*.

10 Continue as #3 through #9 until you reach ½" from the raw edge of the cording.

Covering Raw Edges

11 To cover the raw edges of both ends of the cording, add rows of parallel beads working towards the cut edge. You may need to reduce the number of beads in some rows, ending with the least number of beads in the last row.

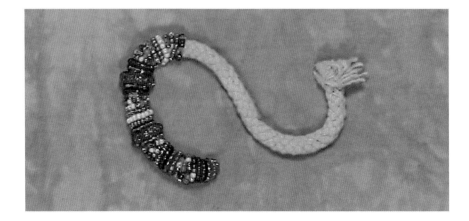

BEADING CONSIDERATIONS

The Beaded Back Stitch, page 20, is used to form letters and words.

1 Portions of a letter that are passed over a second time with a writing instrument are beaded as a single line *(Illustration 2A)*. Then the needle and thread pass through the beads in the line a second time without stitching into the fabric *(Illustration 2B)*. This second pass of the needle and thread will position the needle for beading the next section of the letter (letters "u, n, m," etc.).

2 To maintain control of the bead positions in letters in which horizontal and vertical lines cross, such as the letter "t," the second bead line will not cross over the first bead line. As an example, for the letter "t" bead the vertical lines first, and then bead the horizontal line that crosses the "t." When beading the horizontal line stop at the beaded vertical line, pass the needle and thread through the fabric to the wrong side of the fabric *(Illustration 3C)*. Then, pass the needle and thread through the

fabric to the right side of the fabric on the other side of the vertical line and continue beading the horizontal line *(Illustration 3D)*.

3 To smooth and straighten a completed line of Beaded Back Stitch, see Creating a Smooth Back Stitch, page 19.

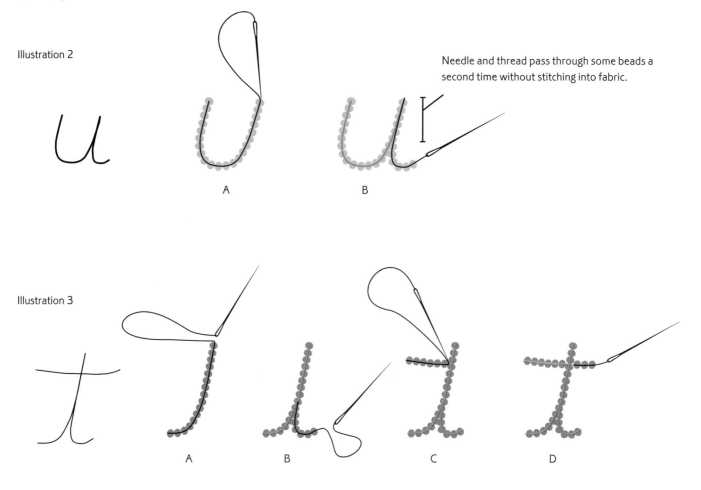

Illustration 2

Needle and thread pass through some beads a second time without stitching into fabric.

A   B

Illustration 3

A   B   C   D

Making a Pattern

1 A letter or word pattern can be hand drawn onto tissue paper, creating a tissue paper beading pattern to follow. Writing directly onto a tissue paper pattern produces beaded letters with a personalized, hand-written look. To construct beaded letters that are uniform both in size and shape, explore fonts and font sizes generated by computer software. After composing the text on the computer screen, print a paper copy. The computer-generated pattern may then be traced to tissue paper or copied onto paper for foundation piecing with a photocopy machine.

2 Cut off excess tissue paper or foundation piecing paper from the perimeter of the pattern, leaving ½" border of paper on all sides of the pattern. Pin the pattern in place on the right side of the fabric.

Beading the Pattern

1 Cut a 2-yard length of Silamide thread. Thread a needle and tie the thread tails together in a knot. You now have a 1-yard length of double thread. Use single thread for size 14° beads.

2 Bead the letters and words using the Beaded Back Stitch, beading through both the paper pattern and fabric. Bead the letters in the same order and direction as if you were hand writing the letters and words.

3 Remove paper pattern from fabric. Use the point of a small scissors, a tweezers, or a pin to remove the paper fibers that are lodged in the corners of the beadwork.

The number of beads on the needle and thread in relationship to the distance between the Stop Beads will determine whether the connecting Elevated Bead Line will be straight or curved.

If the beads on the needle and thread measure the same length as the distance between two Stop Beads, a straight, Elevated Bead Line is constructed. If the length of the beads on the needle and thread measure longer than the distance between two Stop Beads, a curved, Elevated Bead Line is constructed *(Illustration 3)*.

Illustration 3

Length of beads measures the same length as the distance between stop beads

Length of beads measures longer than the distance between stop beads

All Ideas for Elevated Beading configurations were constructed with either the aligned or staggered grid patterns on pages 80–87. For visual clarity, Stop Stitches were constructed in a contrasting color to the Elevated Bead Lines. However, the same bead color could be used for both Stop Stitches and Elevated Bead Lines *(Illustrations 4 thru 7 with photos)*.

Ideas for Elevated Beading

Illustration 4

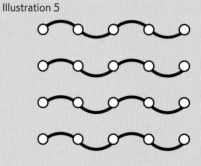

Staggered grid, rotated 90°

Illustration 5

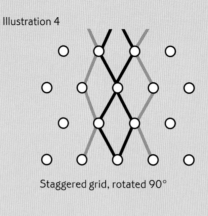

Aligned grid

Illustration 6

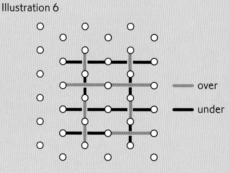

over
under

Staggered grid

Illustration 7

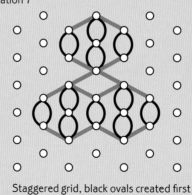

Staggered grid, black ovals created first

Stop stitches shown are size 8°

Stop stitches shown are size 11°

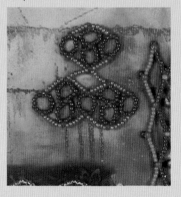

Elevated Beading

1 Use the grid patterns provided on pages 80–87, or draw your own pattern. Patterns should be reproduced on tissue paper or paper for foundation piecing (see Creating Paper Stitch Patterns, page 79). Make an additional photocopy of the pattern on copy paper for sketching your Elevated Beading design.

2 Use the photocopied pattern to sketch the entire design before starting. Note the colors and bead sizes on your sketch for both Stop Stitches and Elevated Bead Lines or use colored pencils.

3 Cut off excess tissue paper or foundation piecing paper from the perimeter of the pattern, leaving ½" border of paper on all sides of the pattern. Pin the pattern in place on the right side of the fabric.

4 Cut a 2-yard length of Silamide thread. Thread a needle and tie the thread tails together in a knot. You now have a 1-yard length of double thread. Using your sketch as a guide, bead all Stop Stitches through the paper pattern and the fabric, with the fabric in an embroidery hoop.

Use Japanese seed beads for Stop Beads if using size 11° or smaller seed beads. The bead holes are larger than Czech beads.

After constructing the last Stop Stitch, the needle and thread will be on the wrong side of the fabric.

5 If the needle and thread are currently under the Stop Stitch where you want to start an Elevated Bead Line, pass the needle through the fabric to the right side of the fabric and up through both beads of the Stop Stitch. If the needle and thread are not in position, make a knot on the wrong side of the fabric and cut off the thread. Then, knot the tails together, and pass the needle through the fabric to the right side of the fabric and up through both beads of any Stop Stitch.

6 The needle and thread are coming out of the Stop Bead of a Stop Stitch. Carefully remove the tissue or paper for foundation piecing pattern from your fabric.

7 Connect the Stop Beads with Elevated Bead Lines, using your sketch as a guide. Upon completing each Elevated Bead Line, pass the needle and thread through both beads of the last connecting Stop Stitch and through the fabric to the wrong side of the fabric with one stitch.

8 Knot the thread on the wrong side of the fabric and cut off excess thread. The Stop Stitches supporting the Elevated Bead Line will be relatively upright with the exception of the first and last Stop Stitch. The end Stop Stitches may bend slightly toward the direction of the Elevated Bead Line (unless the first and last Stop Stitch have been connected by a direct Elevated Bead Line). After

completing a curved Elevated Bead Line, the direction of the curve may be re-directed by hand.

9 Accent beads may be sewn under or next to the Elevated Bead Line pattern (*Photos for Illustrations 4 and 6*).

Elevated Beading may not be appropriate for wearables. The Elevated Bead Lines may catch on objects, which will break the thread, and beaded patterns may shift if brushed against. Elevated Beading processes are more appropriate for art quilts and other display pieces.

Setting a Cabochon with Beads

A cabochon is an object with a flat side (bottom) and a domed side (top). The possibilities are numerous and include: a button without a shank, a cameo, a polished stone cabochon from a rock shop or bead store, or the rounded glass pebbles used for silk floral arrangements.

Supplies:

Background fabric or project on which to bead

Pencil

Embroidery or other small scissors

Optional: embroidery hoop

Beads and Beading Supplies:

Japanese seed beads: size 11° shown

For curved bead lines: see Seed Bead Shape and Color, page 7. Elliptical beads recommended.

Silamide thread: coordinate in color or value with beads

Size 12 Sharps or long beading needle

Stitches:

Fringe, Elevated Beading

Review:

Beading Secrets Revealed, pages 15–17

Overview

Securing a cabochon to fabric with Elevated Beading is similar to constructing Elevated Beading grid patterns, except Beaded Fringe replaces the Stop Stitches.

The cabochon is encircled with short, correctly-spaced Beaded Fringe applied to the fabric surface. The Fringe must be tall enough to bend over the dome edge of the cabochon when the Elevated Bead Line is added. Connecting the Beaded Fringe with short Elevated Bead Lines will hold the cabochon in place. By putting fewer beads on the needle and thread than the distance between the Fringe Stop Beads, and pulling the thread tension tightly, the Fringe will bend and hold the cabochon securely in place on the fabric. No glue will be needed to hold the cabochon on the fabric.

The directions include using a pencil to trace around the perimeter of the cabochon, leaving an outline on the fabric. If you prefer not to mark the fabric, trace around the perimeter of the cabochon on tissue paper using a pencil. Pin the tissue paper to the fabric; follow the instructions as if the cabochon perimeter was traced directly onto the fabric. The tissue paper can be removed with a tweezers when the circle of Fringe is completed, and before the Stop Beads are connected by Elevated Bead Lines.

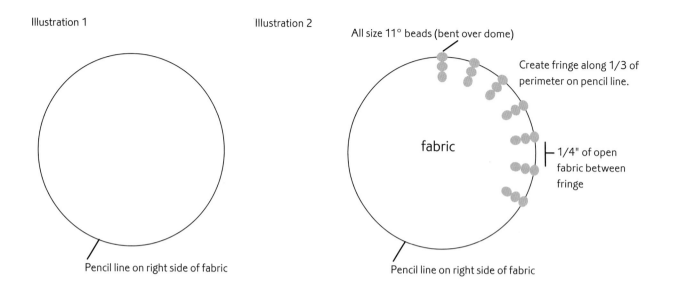

Illustration 1

Pencil line on right side of fabric

Illustration 2

All size 11° beads (bent over dome)

Create fringe along 1/3 of perimeter on pencil line.

fabric

1/4" of open fabric between fringe

Pencil line on right side of fabric

Setting a Cabochon with Beads

1 Cut a 48-inch length of thread. Thread a needle and tie the thread tails together in a knot. You now have a 24-inch length of double thread. Additional thread may be added, but it is easier to learn this technique starting with a length of thread long enough to complete the entire process.

2 Position the cabochon, flat side down, on the right side of the fabric and lightly trace around the perimeter of the cabochon with a pencil. Set the cabochon aside *(Illustration 1)*.

3 For one-third of the way around the perimeter: using the pencil line as a guide, construct Fringe on the line with size 11° beads, leaving ¼" of open fabric between every two Fringe. This is an important measurement *(Illustration 2)*. If the Fringe are placed too close together, they will not hold the cabochon in place when the Elevated Bead Line is added. The height of the Fringe should be tall enough to bend slightly over the dome of the cabochon *(Illustrations 2 and 3)*.

Illustration 3

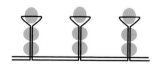

Fringe: number of beads per fringe dependant on shape of cabochon

4 Position the cabochon inside the pencil line. Hold the cabochon in place with your non-beading hand and continue constructing the Fringe around the remaining two-thirds of the perimeter of the cabochon *(Illustration 4)*. Follow the edge of the cabochon, not the pencil line, for Fringe placement. Continue spacing the Fringe with ¼" of open fabric between every two Fringe.

5 After finishing the last Fringe in the circle, the needle and thread are on the wrong side of the fabric. Pass the needle and thread through the fabric to the right side of the fabric and through all the beads of the last Fringe constructed *(Illustration 5)*. The needle and thread are now exiting a Stop Bead. If tissue paper was used as a pattern, remove it now.

Illustration 4

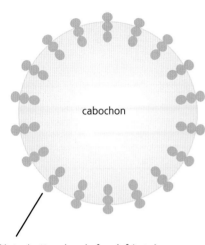

Note: bottom bead of each fringe is now on outer perimeter of cabochon.

Illustration 5

Illustration 6

Illustration 7

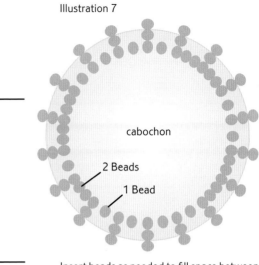

Insert beads as needed to fill space between stop beads. Pull thread tension tightly after the needle and thread pass through each stop bead.

6 Place the cabochon in the center of the circle of Fringe, flat side down on the fabric. On the needle and thread, pick up a length of size 11° seed beads that measure slightly less than the distance to the next Fringe Stop Bead. Pass the needle and thread through the Stop Bead. All Fringe will lay on the cabochon perpendicular to the edge of the cabochon. The number of size 11° seed beads added between Stop Beads is a variable and may not be consistent; the number of beads is determined by the spacing of the Fringe and the height of each Fringe. If you have ¼" of open fabric between each Fringe, probably 0–2 beads will be added between two Stop Beads (*Illustrations 6 and 7*). Form a tight circle of beads as the needle and thread pass through the Stop Bead of each Fringe. The Elevated Bead Line acts as a circular drawstring; pull the thread tension

tightly each time beads are added and the needle passes through the next Stop Bead in the circle.

7 Complete a circle of beads by passing the needle and thread through the first Stop Bead in the circle a second time. If, after pulling the thread tension tightly, the circle of beads is too loose to hold the cabochon in place, some beads between Stop Beads will need to be removed. If thread shows in the circle of beads when the thread tension is pulled tightly, additional beads need to be added to the circle between the Stop Beads. To remove or add beads, pull on the last beads added to the circle, pulling the needle eye out first through the Stop Beads in the circle. Do not push the needle eye first, or push the needle point first through the Stop Beads to remove beads. See Milking the Cow, page 17.

8 After determining the correct number of beads in the circle, pull the thread tension tightly and pass the needle and thread through all of the Stop Beads and Elevated Bead Line beads in the circle a second time.

9 Pull the thread tension tightly again. Pass the needle and thread through all beads in the nearest Fringe and through the fabric under the same Fringe to the wrong side of the fabric with one stitch.

10 Before making a knot, check again for tight thread tension in the beaded circle; very little or no thread should be visible between beads. On the wrong side of the fabric, knot tightly and cut off the needle and thread.

Techniques for Creating a Beaded Kaleidoscope

Adding Elevated Bead Lines

The elevation of the Bead Lines is determined by the height at which they pass through or connect at the Stop Stitch. Following are a number of options for you to consider when designing your own unique Beaded Kaleidoscope. Being aware of options will give you the ability to make each Kaleidoscope a stunning one-of-a-kind creation. Several of the following options will be included in the directions for the Beaded Kaleidoscope, pages 50–51.

Pass Through

2A One Bead Line, passing straight through a Stop Bead.

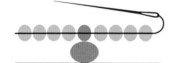

Illustration 2A

2B One Bead Line, passing through a Stop Bead and creating an angle. The degree of angle is dependent on the position of the adjoining Stop Stitch connected by the Bead Line.

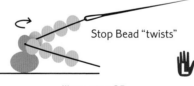

Stop Bead "twists"

Illustration 2B

2C Two Bead Lines passing through and crossing in a Stop Bead.

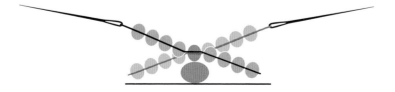

Illustration 2C

Connecting Through Beads and Into Fabric

3D Two Bead Lines entering at opposite sides of the Stop Bead, passing down the Stop Stitch through the fabric to the wrong side of the fabric.

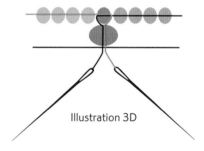

Illustration 3D

3E Two Bead Lines entering at opposite sides of the Stop Stitch, passing down the Stop Stitch through the fabric to the wrong side of the fabric.

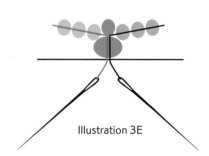

Illustration 3E

Illustration 3D, 3E, and 3F may also be constructed with one needle and thread by taking a stitch in the fabric under the Stop Stitch after completing the first Elevated Bead Line. Pass the needle and thread back through the bead(s) of the same Stop Stitch (and Stop Bead) and in position to continue with the next Elevated Bead Line segment.

Adding a Horizontal Stop Stitch Point

4G One Bead Line, passing through the Stop Bead adding a horizontal Stop Stitch. The needle and thread pass back though the Stop Bead on the Stop Stitch. Continue Bead Line with the same needle and thread. For symmetry, use the same number of beads in both Bead Line segments.

4H One Bead Line, passing through the Stop Bead adding a horizontal Stop Stitch. The needle and thread pass back through the Stop Bead on the Stop Stitch and through the last bead on the Bead Line. Continue Bead Line with the same needle and thread. For symmetry, one additional bead is needed on the first segment of the Bead Line.

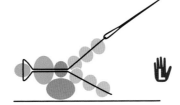

Illustration 4G

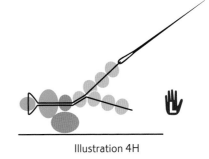

Illustration 4H

3F Two Bead Lines sharing the last Bead on the first Bead Line, connecting in the Stop Bead and passing down the Stop Stitch through the fabric to the wrong side of the fabric. For symmetry, one additional bead is needed on the first Bead Line.

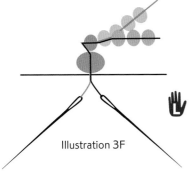

Illustration 3F

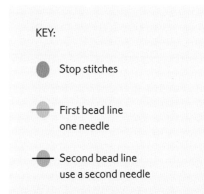

KEY:

● Stop stitches

— First bead line one needle

— Second bead line use a second needle

See pages 92–93 for the left-handed versions of these illustrations.

Entwining Two Bead Lines at an End Point Stop Stitch

51 Using a pattern on pages 88–89, construct two Concentric Circles of Stop Stitches or Stout Fringe

First Bead Line: Rose (in photo), seed beads size 11°

Second Bead Line: Lime (in photo) seed beads size 11°

After determining how many beads to use for the First and Second Elevated Bead Lines, construct all First Bead Lines before constructing the Second Bead Lines even if using the same color beads for both. Note: All beads of a Stop Stitch include the Stop Bead.

First Bead Lines (Rose)

1 Start at Inner Circle Point A, needle and thread passing through all beads of the Stop Stitch, exiting the Stop Bead (*Illustration 5*).

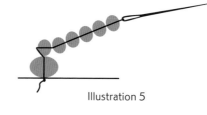

Illustration 5

2 On the needle and thread, pick up a length of size 11° seed beads that measure slightly longer than the distance to Outer Circle Point B (*Illustration 6*).

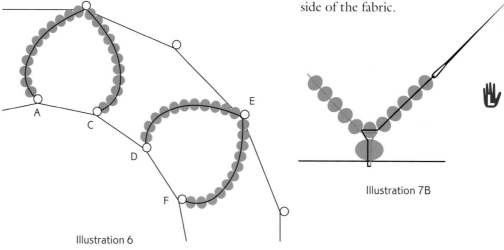

Illustration 6

3 Pass the needle and thread through all beads of the Stop Stitch Point B and through the fabric to the wrong side of the fabric. Pass the needle and thread to the right side of the fabric and through both beads of the Stop Stitch, exiting the Stop Bead (*Illustrations 7A and 7B*).

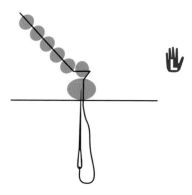

Illustration 7A

4 On the needle and thread, pick up a length of size 11° seed beads that measure slightly longer than the distance to Inner Circle Stop Stitch Point C (*Illustration 6*). Pass the needle and thread through all beads of Stop Stitch Point C and through the fabric to the wrong side of the fabric.

Illustration 7B

 See page 93 for the left-handed version of this illustration.

5 Start at Inner Circle Point D, and then proceed to E and F. Repeat #1 through #4, working clockwise around the two concentric circles *(Illustration 6).*

Second Bead Lines (Lime)

1 *(Illustration 9)* Start at Inner Circle Point A, needle and thread passing through all beads of the Stop Stitch *except* the Stop Bead *(Illustration 8).* Position the needle coming out of the Stop Stitch bead towards the Outer Circle.

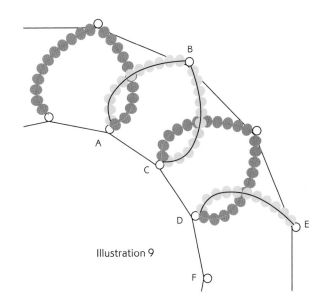

Illustration 9

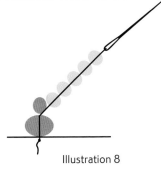

Illustration 8

2 On the needle and thread, pick up a length of size 11° seed beads that measure slightly longer than the distance to Outer Circle Point B *(Illustration 9).* Let the beads fall down to the Stop Stitch at Point A.

3 Wrap the Bead Line from underneath to over the First Bead Line (Rose) near Inner Circle Point A *(Illustration 9).*

4 Pass the needle and thread through all beads of Outer Circle Point B, and through the fabric to the wrong side of the fabric. Pass the needle and thread to the right side of the fabric and through all beads of the Stop Stitch Point B, exiting the Stop Bead *(Illustrations 7A and 7B).*

5 On the needle and thread, pick up a length of size 11° seed beads that measure slightly longer than the distance to Inner Circle Point C. Let the beads fall down to the Stop Bead at Point B *(Illustration 9).*

Wrap the Bead Line over and then under the First Bead Line (Rose). The needle and thread pass through Inner Circle Point C and through the fabric to the wrong side of the fabric. Position the needle going into all beads of the Stop Stitch *except* the Stop Bead, towards the Outer Circle.

6 Start at Inner Circle Point D and proceed to E and F. Repeat #1 through #5, working clockwise around the two concentric circles.

Make only two "Vs" of the First Elevated Bead Lines (Rose) and then make two "Vs" of the Second Elevated Bead Lines (Lime Green). If the Elevated Bead Lines are not pulling each other into "Vs," remove the beads and try again with fewer or more beads.

Putting it All Together: Creating a Beaded Kaleidoscope

The following directions are for the largest Beaded Kaleidoscope on page 42, using the 5 circle grid at 100% (see page 88). Feel free to substitute bead sizes bead colors, Stop Stitch heights, and Elevated Bead Line connections.

Supplies:

Background fabric or project on which to bead

Tissue paper, any color Pigma Micron pen or ultra fine tip permanent marker, and plastic pattern protector
OR
1 sheet of paper for foundation piecing and copy machine

Embroidery hoop

Embroidery or other small scissors

Straight pins

Beads and Beading Supplies:

Seed beads: size 6° and size 11° (Stop Stitches); and size 11° (Bead Lines) shown. Other sizes may be used.

Beads: discs (rondelles), and assorted large beads for accent

For curved bead lines: see Seed Bead Shape and Color, page 7. Elliptical beads recommended.

Silamide thread: coordinate in color or value with beads

Size 12 Sharps or long beading needle

Stitches:

Stop Stitch, Fringe, Elevated Beading

Review:

Beading Secrets Revealed, pages 15–17

Creating Paper Stitch Patterns, page 79

1 Use the 100% grid pattern on page 88. See Creating Paper Stitch Patterns on page 79.

Make an additional photocopy of the pattern on copy paper on which to sketch your design.

2 Cut off excess tissue paper or foundation piecing paper from the perimeter of the pattern, leaving ½" border of paper on all sides of the pattern. Using as few pins as possible, pin the pattern securely in place on the right side of the fabric.

3 Place the fabric, with paper pattern pinned in place, inside an embroidery hoop. Cut a 2-yard length of Silamide thread. Thread a needle and tie the thread tails together in a knot. You now have a 1-yard length of double thread. Construct all Stop Stitches of each circle through the pinned paper pattern and the fabric, using your photocopy sketch as a guide. Remember to knot the thread tails and cut off the thread if a thread stitch on the wrong side of the fabric will be greater than one inch long. See to Knot or Not to Knot, page 17.

4 Stop Stitch/Fringe Supports as Photo, page 42, largest Kaleidoscope. Copy 100% grid, page 88.

Circle 1: Stop Stitch: 6° rose and 11° rose

Circle 2: Fringe: disc clear, 6° rose, 11° rose; alternating with Stop Stitch: disc clear, 11° lime

Circle 3: Fringe: disc clear, 6° dark purple, 11° dark purple

Circle 4: Stop Stitch: 11° light purple, 11° light purple

Circle 5: Stop Stitch: disc clear, 11° orange

5 After constructing the last Stop Stitch, the needle and thread are on the wrong side of the fabric. Make a knot and cut off the thread. Knot the tails together, pass the needle through the fabric to the right side of the fabric and up through all beads of one Circle 1 Stop Stitch. Carefully remove the paper pattern from the fabric.

6 Elevated Bead Lines as Photo, page 42, largest Kaleidoscope.

Circle 1 to Circle 2: rose, First Bead Line; lime, Second Bead line

Start at Circle 1; follow directions as in Entwining Two Bead Lines at an End Point Stop Stitch, pages 46–47.

7 Circle 2 to 3 to 4: dark purple, First Bead Line; light purple, Second Bead Line

Start at Circle 2; follow directions as in Entwining Two Bead Lines at a Midpoint Stop Stitch, pages 48–49.

8 Circle 4 to Circle 5: one Bead Line: orange

Start at Circle 4, needle and thread coming out of the Stop Stitch, not the Stop Bead; construct a bead line that measures the distance clockwise to Circle 5. Pass the needle and thread through the Circle 5 Stop Bead and construct a Stop Stitch (*Illustration 4G*).

9 On the needle and thread, pick up a length of size 11° seed beads that measure the distance clockwise to the next Circle 4 Stop Stitch. Pass the needle and thread through the Stop Stitch and through the fabric to the wrong side of the fabric (*Illustration 3E*) using one needle.

10 Pass the needle through the fabric to the right side of the fabric and back through the same Stop Stitch of Circle 4.

11 Repeat #8 through #10 around concentric Circles 4 and 5.

12 Accent Beads

Within the Beaded Kaleidoscope pattern, accent beads may be sewn directly to the fabric to enhance the pattern and fill in with beaded color.

Designing an Original Kaleidoscope

The circular kaleidoscope grid patterns on pages 88–89 may be enlarged or decreased with a photocopy machine.

Determine the diameter of the kaleidoscope and the number of concentric circles you want to include in the pattern.

Try creating both straight and curved Elevated Bead Line patterns.

Designing Other Patterns Using Kaleidoscope Grid

Using the circular kaleidoscope grid patterns on pages 88–89, experiment by constructing beaded designs other than Kaleidoscopes.

Possible variations include:
Use some but not all Stop Stitch points of the circle grids.
Use some but not all circles of grid.
Use a wedge or half circle of Stop Stitch points on the circle grids.

Large Beaded Images

Supplies:

Background fabric or project on which to bead

Lacy's Stiff Stuff

Pencil

Colored pencils or permanent fabric markers to apply to Stiff Stuff coordinated with bead colors

Small sharp scissors

Embroidery hoop

Beads and Beading Supplies:

Seed beads: size 11° (14° finer detail), to coordinate with pencil or marker colors applied to Stiff Stuff

See Seed Bead Shape and Color, page 7. Elliptical beads recommended.

Silamide thread: coordinate in color or value with beads

Size 12 Sharps or long beading needle

Stitch:

Beaded Back Stitch

Review:

Beading Secrets Revealed, pages 15–17

Large beaded images emerge as dazzling focal points on the surface of art quilts. By applying rows of Beaded Back Stitch firmly to the fabric and tightly against other Beaded Back Stitch rows, a large multi-colored image can be constructed with beads.

Beads versus Thread

A key design consideration for creating a large image with beads instead of embroidery thread is that seed beads are composed of hard glass; embroidery threads are soft and pliable. Unlike embroidery thread, individual glass beads cannot bend to fit into a space, nor blend with another bead color to create a secondary color.

Patterns

The teapot and two other patterns can be found on pages 90–91. Additional sources for large copyright-free patterns suitable for beading are stained glass patterns and coloring books. Whether using a copyright-free pattern or drawing your own pattern:

1. Each section of color or line must be large enough to accommodate a minimum of one row of the Beaded Back Stitch. The smaller the seed bead size, the smaller the area that can be successfully beaded.

2. Draw or choose a relatively simple image, without numerous thin lines or fine detail. Or, simplify an image by mentally removing thin lines and fine detail, and covering these areas with beads.

Opaque Beaded Imagery

Because beads are hard and unyielding, some background fabric will be visible between the rows of Beaded Back Stitch. The eye will perceive the imagery as transparent rather than opaque. Transparent imagery is not a desirable outcome unless you are constructing a ghostly image or a jellyfish. Transparent beaded imagery is especially noticeable if the beads and background fabric are of high contrast in either color or value.

A beaded image will appear opaque if the background fabric is a similar color to the beads placed upon it. Here are three options to achieve beading opacity when creating a large beaded image:

Good: Find the perfect large-scale commercial fabric print in the colors you desire and bead by color, using the fabric as a cue. This requires a long, and usually futile, search for the perfect fabric. Consider simplifying commercial fabric prints by ignoring finer details and covering those areas with a single color of beads.

Better: Design or purchase an appliqué pattern and necessary colors of cotton fabric for the appliquéd imagery. Fuse, machine, or hand appliqué all appliqué pieces in the proper position on a background fabric. Cover the appliqué pieces with coordinating bead colors using the Beaded Back Stitch. A workable option, but a time-consuming preparation process.

Best: Lacy's Stiff Stuff

Preparing the Pattern

1 Using a window or lightbox and a pencil, trace a pattern onto Stiff Stuff. This is a somewhat stiff, white, pressed-fiber sheet approximately 1⁄16" thick.

2 Using colored pencils (or permanent fabric markers if you plan to wash the beading in the future), color each section of the pattern completely with colored pencils, corresponding the pencil color to the approximate color of beads that will be placed on the color. Blue color pencil = any color of blue bead, red color pencil = any color of red bead, etc.

3 If using markers, allow to dry. Cut out the entire pattern on the outer pencil outline, leaving the Stiff Stuff pattern in one piece.

4 With Silamide or sewing thread, hand baste the colored Stiff Stuff pattern to the right side of the background fabric. Baste around the entire colored Stiff Stuff pattern, 1⁄4" in from the edge of the perimeter. The basting stitches will be covered by beads (*Illustration 1*).

5 Cut a 2-yard length of Silamide thread. Thread a needle and tie the thread tails together in a knot. You now have a 1-yard length of double thread.

6 Put the colored Stiff Stuff pattern inside an embroidery hoop. Using the Beaded Back Stitch, bead through the fabric and Stiff Stuff with bead colors that correspond to the colored pencil colors. The Stiff Stuff will remain under the large beaded image after the beading is completed. Before heading, review Creating a Smooth Back Stitch, page 19.

Illustration 1

Stiff Stuff basted to fabric

Beading the Pattern

After reading pages 53–54, you can successfully bead the patterns provided, or any suitable pattern, by following these guidelines:

Bead the smaller sections and lines first (*Illustration 2, example A*). If you leave the small sections until last, the beads from the larger beaded sections will migrate into the smaller sections.

For beading lines that are parallel to the outer edge of a Stiff Stuff pattern; pass the needle through the very edge of the Stiff Stuff (*Illustration 2, example B*).

For beading lines that end at the edge of the Stiff Stuff pattern; pass the needle through the fabric directly where the Stiff Stuff edge ends. The needle will touch the Stiff Stuff edge as it passes through the fabric (*Illustration 2, example C*).

Illustration 2

Beads straddle edge of Stiff Stuff, and needle passes through Stiff Stuff.

B

A

C

Bead smallest segment or line first. Example: veins of a leaf.

At "C" needle passes though fabric at edge of Stiff Stuff.

For a realistic look, work the bead lines in a direction that enhances the perceived shape, dimension, and physical likeness of the object. Only if striving for a folk-art look would you outline a section with beads and fill it in working each row of Beaded Back Stitch inward toward the center.

Color-coded Stiff Stuff pattern

55

Beaded Dragonfly

A popular image in Contemporary, Art Deco, and Japanese design, the appeal of dragonflies is timeless. This beaded dragonfly employs four of the beading stitches from Basic Bead Embroidery & Beyond, pages 19–22.

Supplies:

Background fabric or project on which to add dragonfly

Three 9" squares of tulle (sheerest bridal netting) for wings, your choice of colors

One 9" square of Sulky Solvy or other water-soluble stabilizer

Thin low-loft cotton batting: 3/8" x 1¾"

Dark blue solid or patterned quilt-weight cotton: ½" x 2"

Pigma Micron or ultra fine tip permanent marker, any color

Gold metallic machine embroidery thread

White bobbin thread (extremely fine machine embroidery bobbin thread)

7" embroidery hoop

Embroidery or other small scissors

Metallica 80/12 needle for sewing machine

Straight pins

Review:

Beading Secrets Revealed, pages 15–17

Equipment:

Sewing machine on which the feed dogs can be dropped

Darning foot for sewing machine (preferably clear plastic)

Extension table for the machine bed provided with portable sewing machine

Beads and Beading Supplies:

Seed beads for body: Color A, size 11°; iris or AB blue, dark green, purple, or bronze

Seed beads for tail: Color B, size 6°; iris or AB blue, dark green, purple, or bronze

Seed beads for tail: Color C, size 11°; gold silver-lined

Seed beads for eyes: size 6°; two red

Silamide thread: coordinate in color or value with beads

Size 12 Sharps or long beading needle

Beading Stitches:

Long Stitch
Stop Stitch
Raised Satin Stitch
Back Stitch

Free-Motion Stitching

A sewing machine is needed to construct the dragonfly wings using a free-motion stitching technique. Free-motion stitching relies on your hands moving the fabric in any direction under the needle, not the sewing machine's feed dogs moving the fabric forward under the needle. Think of it as "drawing" stitch lines with the sewing machine needle as your hands move the fabric.

The sewing machine must be well-tuned and lint-free in and around the bobbin case. To perform free-motion stitching, you must be able to drop the feed dogs, or use the plate provided with the sewing machine to cover the feed dogs.

To achieve small thread stitches, the sewing machine needle should move up and down quickly as your hands move the fabric slowly. Strive for many very short stitches. If you do not have experience with free-motion machine stitching, take a free-motion quilting or free-motion embroidery workshop at a quilt shop. There are also several free-motion quilting books available that can teach you the basics.

Wings

1 Layer bottom to top: large section of embroidery hoop, three layers of tulle, water-soluble stabilizer, small section of embroidery hoop (*Illustration 1*).

2 Push the small section of the hoop down over the stabilizer and tulle layers and into the larger section of the hoop. Adjust the tulle and water-soluble stabilizer, removing wrinkles. A few small ripples in the stabilizer will remain. Tighten the screw on the hoop.

Illustration 1

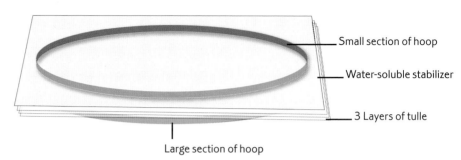

Small section of hoop

Water-soluble stabilizer

3 Layers of tulle

Large section of hoop

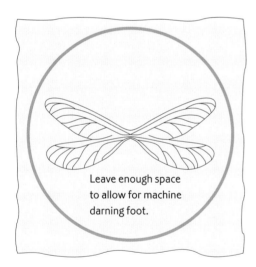

Leave enough space to allow for machine darning foot.

Illustration 2

3 The stabilizer is facing upright, recessed (concave) as you look down into the hoop.

4 Center the hoop over the wing pattern on page 91, with the bottom tulle layer resting on top of the wing pattern. The wing tips must be inward from hoop edges, leaving enough space for the machine darning foot to pass by when stitching (*Illustration 2*). Gently and accurately trace all lines of the wing pattern on to the top of the water-soluble stabilizer with a Pigma Micron or ultra fine permanent marker.

When auditioning color(s) of tulle, lay three layers on top of the right side of the background fabric to determine the color of the completed wings.

Sewing Machine Preparation

Attach extension table provided with portable sewing machine to the machine bed.

Insert Metallica needle.

Use white bobbin thread in bobbin.

Gold metallic thread in top: to prevent the thread from shredding, do not thread last thread guide at the needle.

Loosen top thread tension, for most machines somewhere between 0 and 3.

Set both stitch length and width to 0.

Attach darning foot.

Drop feed dogs.

Put the layers in the hoop under the darning foot, lower the darning foot to down position to engage thread tension.

Occasionally, a sewing machine needle may break while in use. It is recommended that you wear eye protection when using a sewing machine for this or any project.

Free-Motion Stitching

Each time you begin free-motion stitching, take a single stitch and pull up the bobbin thread through all the layers of fabric. This will prevent a "nest" of decorative thread from forming under the fabric layers.

Practice free-motion stitching inside the hoop, in an area away from the wing pattern. The bottom layer of tulle and the large hoop section will both rest directly on the sewing machine bed during free-motion stitching. Mostly gold thread should be visible on the right side of the wings and mostly white bobbin thread on the wrong side of the wings. Check the sewing machine thread tension; and make any top thread tension adjustments as needed until proper thread tension is achieved.

Put the sewing machine needle in the down position into the fabric layers whenever rotating the hoop and/or stopping the sewing machine.

1 Free-motion stitch around the outline of the wings four times, striving for a solid gold outline. Sporadic stitches that stray outward from the pattern outline will be cut off later. Note on the wing pattern *(Illustration 3)* how the outline continues inward, separating the front wings from the back wings; do not overlook this area of the outline as you stitch four times around the perimeter of the wings.

2 Cut off the beginning and ending thread tails close to the fabric layers.

3 Free-motion stitch all internal lines on the wings as one continuous line of stitching. Note that the outer ends of all internal lines touch the stitched outline. Start at the center of the wings, where the body will rest under the wings, Left Front Wing at Point A Front. Stitch a line from Point A to Point B Front, and back over the same internal line from Point B Front to Point C Front. Stitching will pass over each internal line two times. For example, Front Wings: AB, then BC, then CD, then DE, then EF, then FA, then AG, etc. Next, stitch the internal lines on the Right Front Wing.

4 Stitch the internal lines on the Left Back Wing: AB, BC, CD, DE, EF, FE, EG, GH, etc. Repeat for the Right Back Wing.

Illustration 3

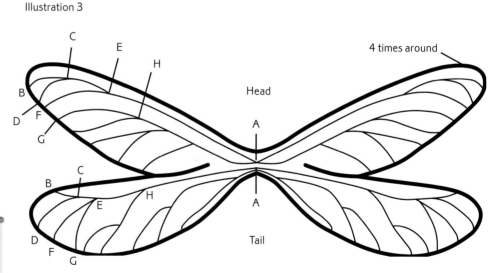

5 Remove the hoop from the sewing machine bed. Cut thread tails close to the fabric layers, and remove all layers from hoop. With embroidery scissors, carefully cut though the stabilizer and the tulle layers as closely as possible to the outer perimeter of the solid gold thread outline around the wings. Cut off any obvious stray thread stitches.

6 Using one hand, press the wings flat on your other hand, while rinsing the wings in warm water to remove water-soluble stabilizer. Keeping the wings flat, blot between paper towels until dry. Trim away any stray gold thread from around the perimeter of the wings. Set wings aside.

Fabric Armature for Beaded Body

A padded form, or fabric armature, will provide a realistic three-dimensional body shape for the dragonfly. When the beaded dragonfly is completed, the fabric armature will be completely covered with beads.

1 Cut a ⅜" x 1¾" piece of thin cotton batting. Trim one end to a point as illustrated (*Illustration 4*).

Illustration 4

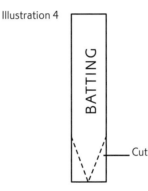

Cut

2 Center batting on wrong side of dark blue ½" x 2" fabric (*Illustration 5*).

Illustration 5

3 Fold the fabric over the batting at the blunt end of the batting and hold in place (*Illustration 6*).

Illustration 6

Fold toward you.

4 Fold the batting/fabric, bringing the long raw edges of the wrong side of the fabric together. Using Silamide or sewing thread, hand stitch small overhand stitches to hold the raw fabric edges together. When the beaded dragonfly is finished, the overhand stitched fabric raw edges will be hidden between the dragonfly body and the background fabric. Start at the head and stitch down the body, stopping at where the batting was trimmed to a point (*Illustration 7*). The head will be flat on the short end due to folding in the short edge of fabric in #3.

Illustration 7

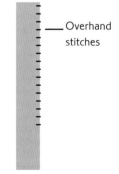

Overhand stitches

5 Continue to overhand stitch down the body towards the batting point. When you reach the beginning of the trimmed batting point, fold and cross the raw edges of fabric firmly around the batting toward the center. The long raw edges of fabric will overlap creating a padded point. Continue stitching, keeping the padded point in place *(Illustration 8)*. After the last stitch, knot the thread tight to the padded point and cut off the remaining thread and needle.

Illustration 8

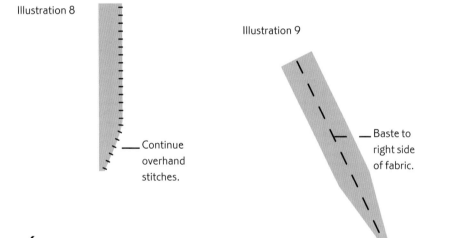

—— Continue overhand stitches.

6 Lay the body, seam down, in place on the background fabric. Leave room for a long beaded tail and the dragonfly wings that will be attached later. Hand baste the body in place with a few long basting stitches down the center of the entire length of the padded body. The basting stitches pass through

the body and the background fabric *(Illustration 9)*. Knot the thread tight to the wrong side of the background fabric. Cut off the remaining thread and needle.

7 After basting in place, "plump" up the entire length of the body by squeezing the long sides of the body between the thumb and index finger. Move your fingers down the length of the body, from the head to the padded point. The body should now be somewhat round, not flat.

Illustration 9

—— Baste to right side of fabric.

Beaded Eyes

1 Cut a 2-yard length of Silamide thread. Thread a needle and tie the thread tails together in a knot. You now have a 1-yard length of double thread.

2 Long Stitch three size 11° seed beads Color A to background fabric centered in front of and touching the flat head end *(Illustration 10)*. The beaded eyes, which will be attached to the flat head end, will rest on top of this row of beads. This Long Stitch will support the eyes parallel to the background fabric, allowing the dragonfly eyes to look forward, not downward.

Illustration 10

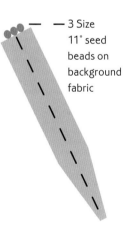

—— 3 Size 11° seed beads on background fabric

Illustration 11

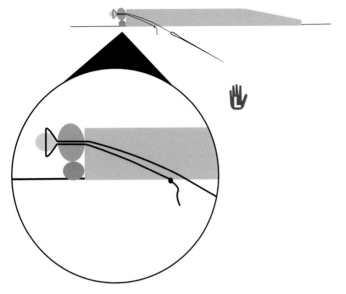

3 Pass needle and thread through the background fabric, at an angle through the head and out the flat end of the head parallel to background fabric. The needle exits the head where the first of two eyes will be placed *(Illustration 11)*.

4 On the needle, pick up a red size 6° and a Color A size 11°. Let the beads fall down the thread to the flat end of the head. Pass the needle back through the red size 6°, into the flat end of the head, passing at an angle downward through the head and the background fabric to the wrong side of the fabric. The first eye is resting on the Long Stitch from #1 *(Illustration 11)*.

5 For the second eye, repeat #3 through #4.

Beaded Head

Raised Satin Stitch: size 11° seed beads Color A

The padded body will be covered by parallel rows of Beaded Raised Satin Stitch, starting at the head and ending at the tip of the padded point.

For the entire length of the body, the roundness of the girth will be maintained by the needle position each time the needle passes though the background fabric. The needle will pass through the background fabric slightly under the body to the right side of fabric before adding beads to the needle and thread. After the correct number of beads

in the Satin Stitch is determined by measuring around the girth with a length of beads on the thread, the needle will pass through the background fabric to the wrong side of the fabric slightly under the body.

The first Satin Stitch will wrap around the head end of the body, pushed snug against the area where the eyes connect to the head *(Illustration 12)*.

1 Insert the background fabric, with attached fabric armature, in the hoop.

Pass the needle and thread through the background fabric to the right side of the background fabric, exiting slightly under the side just behind the flat end of the padded head *(Illustration 12, Point A)*.

2 On the needle and thread, pick up the number of beads that will cover the girth of the padded head. Wrap this row of beads over the padded head to determine the correct number of beads to use *(Illustration 12)*.

3 After the correct number of beads are on the thread, pass the needle and thread slightly under the opposite side of the head through the background fabric to the wrong side of the background fabric *(Illustration 12, Point B)*.

4 Repeat #1 through #3, constructing two more Satin Stitches over the head area, for a total of three parallel rows of beads *(Illustration 13)*.

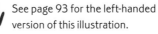 See page 93 for the left-handed version of this illustration.

Attaching Wings

Raised Satin Stitch: size 11° seed beads Color A

Using one straight pin, pin the wings in place on the body directly behind and touching the last of the three rows of beads wrapped around the head. Check that the gold metallic thread is up on the wings and that the front wing tips are pointing forward towards the dragonfly head.

Dragonfly wings rest on top of the insect's back, they do not come out of the insect's sides. Be careful to keep the wings parallel to the background fabric so they appear to be resting on the insect's back, not bent downward around the body. To hold the wings in position behind the head, the body sections under the wings and the top of the wings on the back section will be covered with beads.

1 Continuing with parallel rows of beads, pass the needle and thread through the fabric to the right side of the background fabric, exiting slightly under the edge of the padded body, directly behind and touching the last row of beads wrapped around the padded head.

2 On the needle and thread, pick up the number of beads (approximately three) that will wrap ⅓ of the girth and measure to underside of the midpoint section of the wings (*Illustration 14*). Keeping the beads tight against the padded body, pass the needle and thread through the

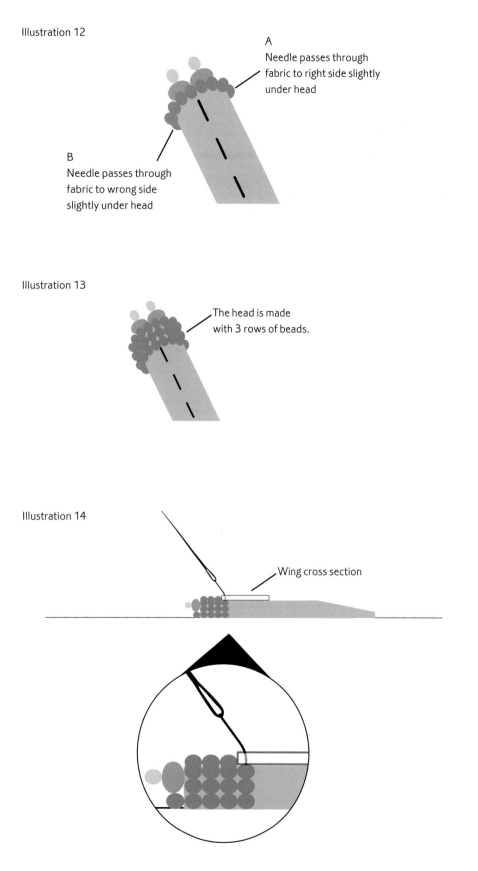

Illustration 12

A
Needle passes through fabric to right side slightly under head

B
Needle passes through fabric to wrong side slightly under head

Illustration 13

The head is made with 3 rows of beads.

Illustration 14

Wing cross section

Illustration 15

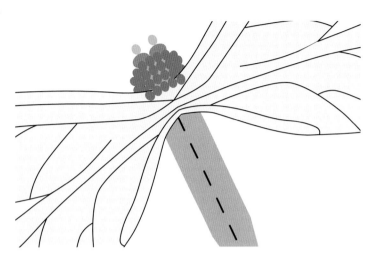

Beaded Body

Raised Satin Stitch: size 11° seed beads Color A

Continue covering the body girth with wrapped parallel rows of Satin Stitches *(Illustration 16)*. Where the body starts to taper towards the padded point, reduce the number of beads accordingly. The last row at the tip of the padded point will be a Satin Stitch of three beads.

Beaded Tail

Back Stitch: seed beads size 6° Color B, seed beads size 11° Color C gold silver-lined

The tail of a dragonfly is longer than the body; it may be straight or curved. Depending on the length and direction of the tail, the fabric may be repositioned in the hoop, or removed from the hoop.

wings at the edge of the body where the wings are resting. The needle passes through the wings perpendicular to the background fabric and the wings.

3 On the needle and thread, pick up the number of beads (approximately five) that will cover only the section of wings resting on the padded body back. These beads touch and are parallel to the third row of beads on the head *(Illustration 15)*. Measure the length of beads on top of the midpoint section of the wings on the body back for accuracy, and pass the needle and thread through only the wings, perpendicular to the background fabric and wings.

4 On the needle and thread, pick up the number of beads (approximately three) that will wrap around the remaining ⅓ of the girth. Keeping the beads tight against the

padded body and touching the third row of beads on the head, pass the needle and thread through the background fabric to the wrong side of the fabric slightly under the body.

5 Satin Stitches will cover the midpoint section of the wings resting on the padded body back and under the wings on both sides of the body. Repeat #1 through #4 for each row of beads until parallel rows of beads cover the entire wing section on the back.

Illustration 16

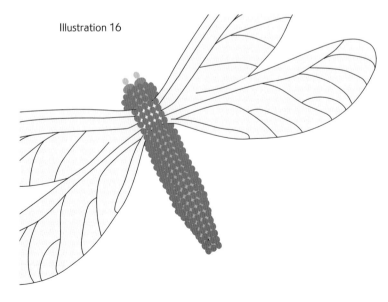

1 Pass the needle and thread to the right side of the fabric and into the padded body near the point end. Angle the needle so the needle exits the very tip of the padded point in the center of the Satin Stitch circle of three beads, parallel to the background fabric *(Illustration 17)*.

2 Put a size 6° seed bead, a size 11°, and a size 6° on the needle, constructing the tail with the Back Stitch *(Illustration 17)*. Alternate between size 6° and size 11° seed beads, applied in three bead increments *(Illustrations 18A–18C)*. End the tail with a size 11° seed bead. Knot the thread tight to the wrong side of the background fabric. Cut off the remaining thread and needle.

3 If the fabric is in a hoop, remove it.

Finishing Touches

1 Check again for stray gold threads and cut them off of the wings.

2 The dragonfly wing tips may curl up away from fabric; to prevent this, make a small hidden thread stitch at the tip of each wing. For each wing, make a thread stitch passing through the fabric directly under the wing tip to the right side of the fabric, through the edge of the wing tip, and directly under the wing tip through the fabric to the wrong side of the fabric.

Illustration 17

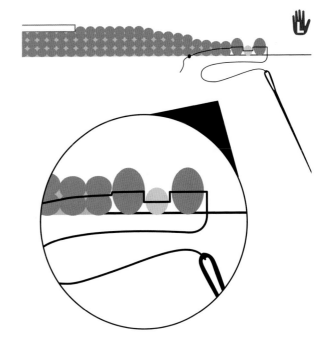

Illustration 18

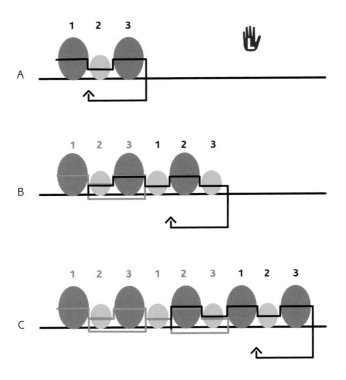

 See page 93 for the left-handed version of this illustration.

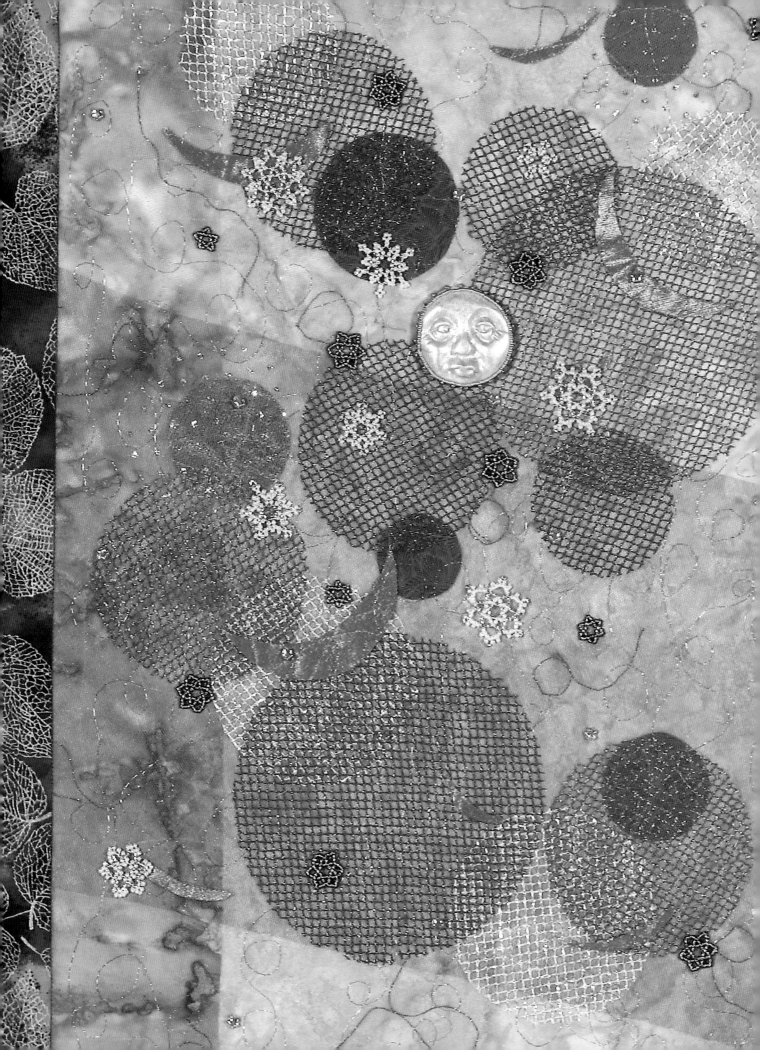

Beaded Snowflakes & Stars

These elegant beaded snowflakes are created using a needlewoven beadwork technique. With needle, thread, and beads, each snowflake is individually constructed in your hands. When completed, you may attach the snowflakes to an art quilt or other fabric project.

Supplies:

Background fabric or project on which to attach finished Snowflakes or Stars

Embroidery or other small scissors

Beads and Beading Supplies:

Japanese seed beads size 11°. Two colors of white, or white and clear AB.

See Seed Shape and Color, page 7. Elliptical beads recommended.

Silamide thread: natural or white

Stars: gold size 11° seed beads, gold thread

Size 12 Sharps or long beading needle

Thread Tension:

Tight thread tension is needed. After adding beads, the needle and thread pass through an existing bead in the snowflake. Give the thread a strong tug at the point where it exits the existing bead. Tug holding the thread, not the needle.

Overview

When you feel confident creating snowflakes, one bead color can be used for the entire snowflake. The illustrations and directions use two colors of beads as a teaching tool. For instructional purposes, the two colors of beads are identified as light and dark beads.

Star Variation

After completing Row 2 or Row 3, See Knotting Instructions, page 69.

Making the Snowflake

1 Cut a 3-yard length of Silamide thread. Thread the needle and make the tails even, but do not tie the thread tails together in a knot. Pick up 12 beads on the needle and thread. Start with a light bead and end with a dark bead alternating between the two colors. Let the beads fall down the thread, leaving a 3" double tail.

2 Row 1: Hold the tails in one hand approximately 3" from the end of the tails and the other end of the thread in your second hand just after Bead 12. Make a square knot leaving 3" tails; pull the thread tightly to secure the knot (*Illustration 1*). No thread should be visible between the beads in the circle.

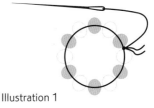

Illustration 1

3 Pass the needle and thread counter clockwise through 2 beads, coming out of a light bead at the top of the circle (*Illustration 2*).

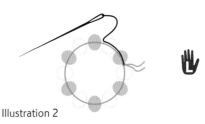

Illustration 2

Art quilt and beading
by Nancy Eha

 See page 94 for the left-handed version of this illustration.

67

4 Row 2: Pick up on the needle and thread 3 beads: light, dark, light. Let the 3 beads fall down the thread to the beadwork. Working counter clockwise, pass the needle and thread through the next light bead in Row 1 *(Illustration 3)*. Repeat a total of six times working counter clockwise around the circle with tight thread tension. The * in Illustration 4 indicates the last light bead the needle passes through to finish Row 2.

Illustration 3

5 Pass needle and thread through the first 2 beads of Row 2, a light bead and then a dark bead. The needle is exiting a dark bead in Row 2 *(Illustration 4)*. The needle has taken a "step up" in Row 2, in preparation to start Row 3.

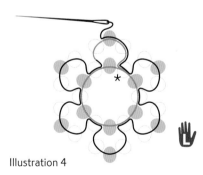

Illustration 4

6 Row 3: Pick up on the needle and thread 5 beads: two light, one dark, two light. Let the 5 beads fall down the thread to the beadwork.

Working counter clockwise pass the needle and thread through the dark bead on the next tip *(Illustration 5)*. Repeat a total of six times working counter clockwise around the circle with tight thread tension. The * in Illustration 6 indicates the last dark bead the needle passes through to finish Row 3.

Illustration 5

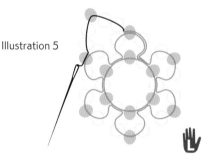

7 "Step up" by passing the needle and thread through the first 3 beads of Row 3, ready to start Row 4. The needle is now exiting a dark bead *(Illustration 6)*. For a smaller snowflake, skip Row 4 and continue with Snowflake Design Options, page 69.

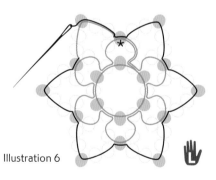

Illustration 6

8 Row 4: Pick up on the needle and thread 7 beads: three light, one dark, three light. Let the 7 beads fall down the thread to the bead-work. Working counter clockwise pass the needle and thread through the dark bead on the next tip

(Illustration 7). Repeat a total of six times, working counter clockwise around the circle with tight thread tension. The * in *Illustration 8* indicates the last dark bead the needle passes through to finish Row 4.

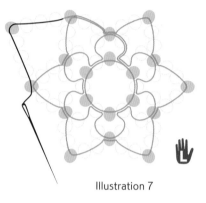

Illustration 7

9 "Step up" by passing the needle and thread through the first 1 or more beads Row 4. The last bead the needle passes through will be the position of the first design element in Row 5 *(Illustration 8)*.

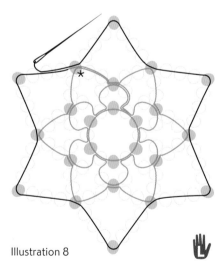

Illustration 8

See page 94 for the left-handed version of this illustration.

Snowflake Design Options

The needle is now exiting a bead in Row 4, add a design element, and then pass the needle through more beads in Row 4 until the needle and thread reach the position for another design element. Do this for each of the six large points of the snowflake. Add all design elements in one pass around the perimeter of the snowflake, as the bead holes are filling with thread and may not allow you to come back for a second pass. The design options can be used in many combinations, but space the design elements no closer than every other bead of Row 4. You may need to "primp" each design element with your hands after constructing to match the illustrations. Continue with tight thread tension.

1 = Bead on snowflake in last row

Illustration 9A
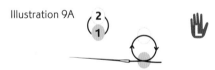

Clockwise thread circle connecting 2 beads (*Illustration 9A*).

Illustration 9B
Clockwise thread circle connecting 4 beads (*Illustration 9B*).

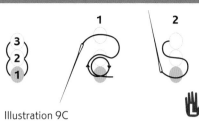
Illustration 9C

(*Illustration 9C*)

1. Clockwise thread circle connecting Beads 1 and 2, passing through Bead 2 again. Add Bead 3.
2. Counter clockwise half thread circle passing through Bead 2, clockwise half thread circle passing through Bead 1.

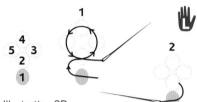
Illustration 9D

(*Illustration 9D*)

1. Counter clockwise thread circle adding Beads 2, 3, 4 and 5, passing through Bead 2 again.
2. Clockwise half thread circle passing through Bead 1.

Knotting Instructions

1 When the Snowflake or Star is completed, wherever the needle and thread are exiting the beadwork, there is an additional set of threads or a thread "bridge" between two beads. Pry the two beads slightly apart with the needle and lay the needle under the thread "bridge" (*Illustration 10A*).

Illustration 10A   Illustration 10B

2 Hold the needle and pull it and the attached thread slowly under and away from the "bridge" until a 2" to 3" loop of thread appears. Pass the needle and thread through the loop of thread and keep pulling the needle until a tight knot is formed on the thread "bridge" (*Illustration 10B*).

3 Repeat #1 through #2 a second time under the same thread "bridge." This finishes the knot.

4 Pass the needle through 1 bead on either side of the knot, and then through the next 3–4 beads in Row 4. Pull the thread tension tight, and cut off excess thread and needle.

5 Thread tails from Row 1: one tail at a time, thread a tail into a needle and pass the tail through 4 beads in Row 1. Pull the thread tension tight, and cut off excess thread and needle.

Attaching to Fabric

The small stitches made to attach snowflakes or stars to fabric should not be visible.

Snowflake: lay snowflake flat on fabric; take a tiny thread stitch through the fabric to the right side of fabric and though the outermost tip of each large point, repeat for each added design element.

Star: lay star flat on fabric; take a tiny thread stitch through the fabric to the right side of fabric and through the outermost tip of each large point.

Constructing a Beaded Art Quilt

An art quilt is a wall hanging, not a quilt for warmth on a bed or a lap. Most art quilts fit the traditional quilt description of having three layers that are attached together—the quilt top, batting, and the quilt back. The three layers may be tied together with knotted thread, stitched together, or fused together with iron on fusible web. The weight of a beaded art quilt may cause the art quilt top to sag when hung, unless all three quilt layers are secured together in some manner.

Creating the Quilt Top

The first step in making an art quilt is creating the quilt top. There are no rules to follow and the possibilities are infinite. The shape does not need to be square, rectangle, symmetrical, have straight edges, or even be two-dimensional. The use of any and all fabrics, notions, and even found objects is acceptable. The top may be a whole cloth quilt using only one piece of fabric, or cut fabric pieces stitched, fused, or otherwise held together to make a larger piece of fabric from smaller pieces. The fabric surface may be altered by dyeing, scrunching, folding, slashing, layering, or fusing fabric shapes. The quilt top may be further embellished by painting, stamping, foiling, applying printed images or photos, hand or machine stitching, beading, etc. A condensed definition of an art quilt could be: a quilt + original design = art quilt. Remember, an art quilt comes from your creative self; there are no wrong answers!

Beading the Quilt Top

The easiest point in the construction sequence to add beading is after all three quilt layers are secured together, but before the hanging sleeve and label are added. By waiting until this point in the construction process, the finished quilt will serve as a firm foundation on which to bead, and reduce the risk of the quilt top puckering from the beading stitches. However, all the beading thread stitches will show on the quilt back. Ask yourself, "Do I care?"

Quilters love to look at quilt backs to see the patterns that hand or machine quilting stitches make. At every quilt show "white glove" volunteers are kept busy turning over the quilts for quilters who want to admire the quilt backs. (They know better than to touch with bare hands, as body oils and grime may be left on the quilts.) Do you plan to enter the beaded art quilt in a judged show?

Hand quilters know a technique to hide thread knots and thread stitches between quilt layers. Unfortunately, this is a very difficult task with most beading stitches. My advice: if you do not want to see beading stitches on the quilt back, do not bead as one of the final steps of construction. Instead, use the following construction sequence, Facing a Quilt. Not only will the beading thread and knots be hidden between layers, but all three quilt layers will be secured firmly together. This is also is an easy way to finish an art quilt without adding binding.

Supplies:

Unbeaded art quilt top

Hobbs Heirloom 80/20 Fusible batting
OR
Flannel 2" wider and longer than quilt top

If using flannel: masking tape, sewing thread, and needle

Backing fabric: size of quilt top

Hanging sleeve fabric: 10½" x width of quilt top

Pellon Wonder Under fusible web: size of quilt back

Teflon press cloth

Iron

Fabric scissors

Embroidery or other small scissors

Rotary cutter, rotary ruler, and rotary mat for cutting fabric

Straight pins

Sewing machine

Lattice board for hanging quilt

Beads and Beading Supplies:

Beads: any size or assorted sizes of seed beads and other beads

Silamide thread: coordinate in color or value with beads

Size 12 Sharps or long beading needle

Before Beading

1 Construct the art quilt top, including borders. Cut Hobbs Heirloom 80/20 Fusible batting or flannel (in place of batting) 1" larger than the quilt top on all edges.

2 Lay batting flat for 24 hours or longer before using. Press quilt top and flannel. With right side of quilt top up, center quilt top on top of the batting or flannel. Smooth both layers flat as you center.

3 Hobbs Heirloom 80/20 Fusible batting: with iron, fuse to wrong side of quilt top as per directions on package.

Flannel: using masking tape, tape both layers to a table top. Baste by hand with a long running stitch through both layers in a 3" square grid, using a single strand of sewing thread (*Illustration 1*). Make sure a line of basting is stitched ¼" in from all raw edges of the quilt top. Remove all masking tape.

> If you are making a garment or project that will be washed, pre-wash all fabric, flannel, or batting. For garments, Hobbs Thermore is a good choice as it is low loft batting that drapes well on the body and does not shrink when washed.

Beading and Quilting

Steps #1 and #2 may be done in reverse order.

1 Bead through the two layers, beading no closer than ½" from quilt top raw edges. With beading in place, approximately a ½" clearance will be needed to trim raw edges and sew a connecting ¼" seam. After sewing the connecting seam, you may go back and spot bead as needed. The beading knots and thread stitches will show on the back side of the batting/flannel, but will be covered by the quilt back.

2 Machine or hand quilt through the two layers. It is amazing how close to beading you can machine quilt as the presser foot will gently push beads away from the needle. With a ¼" presser foot or darning foot, machine quilting may be stitched up to ⅛" from beading. If quilting by machine, be careful not to stitch over beads. If the needle comes in contact with glass beads, the beads will break. Always wear eye protection when operating a sewing machine.

Blocking the Quilt

After beading and quilting, the quilt may no longer lay flat or the edges may have pulled inward. The quilt may need to be blocked, or "coaxed," back to its original shape.

1 Lightly spray the back side of the batting/flannel evenly with water. Avoid spraying water directly on the beads on the quilt top. Fusible batting may lift off the quilt top in large areas not beaded or quilted.

2 With the right side of the quilt top up, generously pin all four quilt top edges through the batting/flannel and into a design wall or clean bulletin board. A tight weave carpet may also be used. Work outward, pinning opposite edges first. When all edges are pinned, some areas may need to be stretched and pinned again to achieve the original size and shape. Leave the quilt top pinned in place 48 hours to dry. Blocking may be repeated if necessary.

Illustration 1

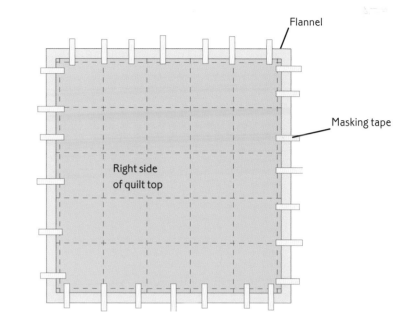

Flannel

Right side of quilt top

Masking tape

Illustration 2

Practice the facing sequence with a 12" x 12" piece of fabric of a similar weight as your quilt top, batting/flannel, and backing.

Facing a Quilt

1 Square up the corners and edges of the quilt top and trim excess batting/flannel with a rotary ruler and rotary cutter on a rotary cutting mat. Leave as much of the ½" unbeaded fabric on all edges as possible to accommodate the addition of the ¼" facing seam around the perimeter of the quilt (*Illustration 2*).

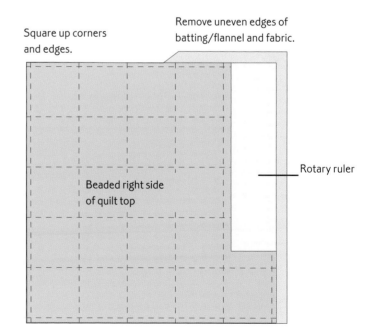

Square up corners and edges.

Remove uneven edges of batting/flannel and fabric.

Beaded right side of quilt top

Rotary ruler

Illustration 3

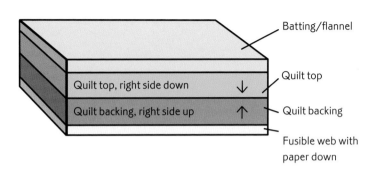

Batting/flannel

Quilt top

Quilt top, right side down ↓

Quilt backing, right side up ↑

Quilt backing

Fusible web with
paper down

Illustration 4

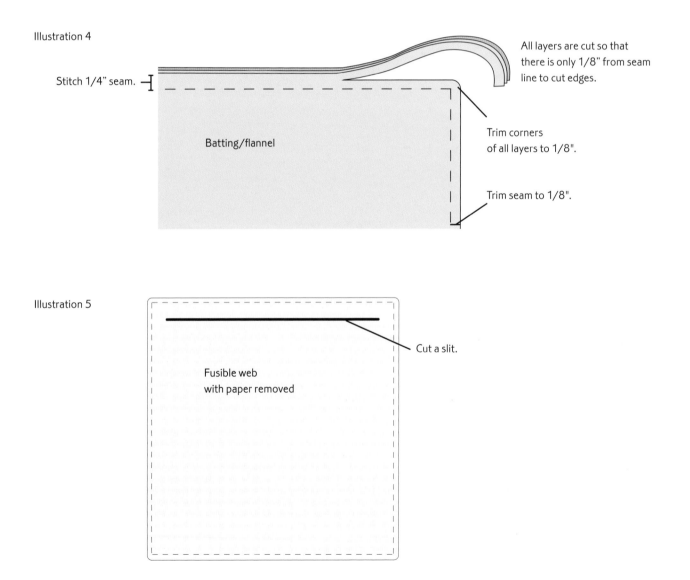

All layers are cut so that
there is only 1/8" from seam
line to cut edges.

Stitch 1/4" seam.

Batting/flannel

Trim corners
of all layers to 1/8".

Trim seam to 1/8".

Illustration 5

Cut a slit.

Fusible web
with paper removed

2 Measure the quilt top. Cut the quilt backing and Pellon Wonder Under fusible web ¼" shorter in both width and length than the quilt top. For large quilts, several lengths of fusible web will be needed. Use backing fabric that is the same or a similar color as the quilt top raw edges.

3 Using a Teflon pressing sheet (also known as Teflon press cloth) to protect the iron, press the wrong side of backing fabric to the fusible web following the web manufacturer's directions. Do not remove the paper backing on the fusible web.

4 Lay the right side of the quilt top on top of the right side of the quilt back *(Illustration 3)*. (Right sides together, fusible web paper downward.) Using a generous number of straight pins, securely pin all layers every ½" on all four edges.

5 Place paper of fusible web down on the sewing machine, batting/flannel up, machine stitch a ¼" seam using a ¼" presser foot or zipper presser foot around the quilt perimeter. You may also securely hand stitch this seam. Trim all layers to a ⅛" seam allowance. Trim the corners of all layers as illustrated *(Illustration 4)*. Remove paper from the fusible web.

6 Very carefully, so as not to cut the quilt top, cut a 10" long slit (shorter for narrower quilts) with scissors through only the backing, approximately 3" down from the top edge of the quilt. The slit is cut near the top of the quilt; the hanging sleeve on the finished quilt will cover it *(Illustration 5)*.

7 Turn the quilt inside out *(Illustration 6)*. With an awl, dull pencil, or other pointed instrument inserted, gently push out the corners until square. With the right side of the seam upward, lay the seam open on the table and run a finger firmly and slowly down the length the seam line. Continue to "finger press" the seam around the entire perimeter of the quilt.

8 Remove all basting stitches.

9 Following the fusible web manufacturer's directions, fuse the backing fabric to batting/flannel with an iron. First, press the edges at the seams on the back side of the quilt, pulling the back so that the seam sewn in #5 is on the quilt edge where the quilt top and back meet. Once the edges are straight and the corners square, iron inward. The edges of the cut slit should meet and be sealed in place. This step secures all three layers together, and eliminates any possibility of the quilt top sagging from the weight of beads when hung on a wall.

Illustration 6

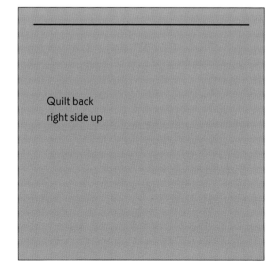

Quilt back
right side up

Turn quilt inside-out,
end with quilt back facing you.

Label

Sew or fuse a cloth label on the backing near the bottom with the quilt title, your name, and date.

Sleeve for Hanging

To display an art quilt on a wall, a hanging sleeve is attached to the back of the quilt. Cylindrical poles are used for hanging quilts at most quilt shows. The following directions add a small amount of slack in the sleeve to accommodate a pole. When hanging a quilt on a wall, a length of hidden lattice board is inserted into the sleeve. The extra fabric allowance for a pole will not be noticeable when a lattice board is used.

1 Cut a piece of backing fabric 1" shorter than the finished width of the quilt x 10½". This allows for a ¼" double hem on each end and positions the finished sleeve 1" in from each vertical edge of the quilt. On both of the 10½" raw edges, fold the edges ¼" toward the wrong side of the fabric and press. Fold the 10½" edges again ¼" toward the wrong side of the fabric and press again *(Illustration 7)*.

2 With a straight machine stitch or by hand, stitch the hems created in #1.

3 With right sides of fabric together, fold the fabric in half, raw edges matching on top of each other. Sew the raw edges together with a ¼" seam *(Illustration 8)*. Turn the tube inside out, with the right side of fabric showing.

4 Press the sleeve so the long seam is at the midpoint of one long side of the sleeve. The long seam of the sleeve will be hidden against the back of the quilt. When the sleeve is sewn to the backing, it will cover the slit you cut open and fused shut.

5 With the sleeve seam side down on the quilt back, center and place the sleeve ¾" down from the top edge of the quilt back. Pin only the top fold of the sleeve in place. With small stitches, hand stitch the top folded sleeve edge to the quilt back and batting layers. When sewing a hanging sleeve in place on a large or heavy quilt, every fourth stitch should go through all three layers *(Illustration 9)*.

6 Remove all pins. Keeping the sleeve flat on the quilt back, roll the top of the sleeve upward until the new sleeve top edge is now ¼" from the quilt back top edge. Keeping the sleeve in this position, pin the bottom edge of the sleeve in place. With small stitches, hand stitch the bottom folded sleeve edge to the quilt back and batting layers. If the quilt is large or heavy, every fourth stitch should go through all three layers *(Illustration 10)*.

Illustration 7
Sleeve for Hanging

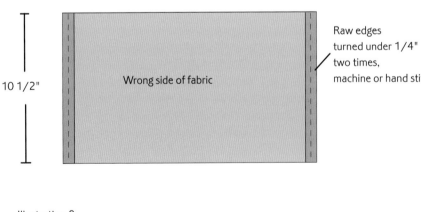

10 1/2"

Wrong side of fabric

Raw edges turned under 1/4" two times, machine or hand stitch

Illustration 8

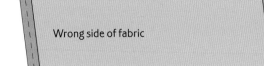

Wrong side of fabric

Fold in half

Illustration 9

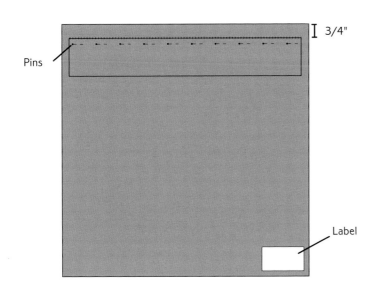

Pins

3/4"

Label

Illustration 10

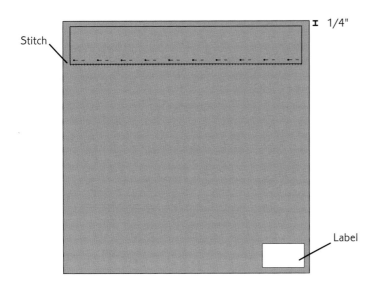

Stitch

1/4"

Label

Hanging the Quilt

1 Purchase ¼" by 1⅛" lattice board from a hardware store or lumber yard. Cut lattice board into a length that is 1" longer than the sleeve on the quilt.

2 Drill holes for small nails approximately ¼" in from two corners on the same long edge of the lattice board. The holes should be large enough for a small nail head to pass through.

3 Insert the cut lattice board into the sleeve, the drilled holes towards top edge of the finished quilt. Have someone hold the quilt on a wall for positioning. With a pencil, mark on the wall the placement of two nails that will correspond to the two drilled holes in the lattice board.

4 Hammer nails in place on the wall. With the lattice board in the quilt sleeve, slip the drilled holes over the nail heads to hang the quilt.

For art quilts with Beaded Coils or large areas of raised beading, facing the quilt may be difficult. Instead, fuse the backing directly to the batting/flannel and add binding.

Creating Paper Stitch Patterns

Overview

For precise positioning of beading stitches without marking on the fabric, some beading techniques require the construction of a paper stitch pattern. The paper stitch pattern is pinned to the right side of the fabric. It is easy to place the beading stitches on the fabric in the desired location by beading through both the fabric and paper pattern. The paper pattern must be on a paper that tears away easily after the beading is completed, leaving no trace to indicate a pattern was used as a beading guide. Two pattern-making techniques follow; one using tissue paper and one using paper for foundation piecing.

Copying Patterns to Paper

Tissue Paper

Tissue paper cannot be sent through a copy machine, therefore tissue paper patterns must be hand traced. Place a single layer of relatively wrinkle-free white or pastel tissue paper on top of the pattern. Insert a piece of clear plastic between the pattern and the tissue paper. A single layer of plastic from a plastic page protector for a three-ring binder works well. The plastic serves as a pattern protector, it will prevent ink from going through the tissue paper onto the pattern.

Using a Pigma Micron pen or sharp pencil, trace the pattern onto the tissue paper. Trace with a light pressure so that the pen or pencil does not tear the tissue paper. Cut off the excess tissue paper from around the pattern leaving ½" margin of paper. Using pins sparingly, pin the pattern in place on the fabric or art quilt.

Paper for Foundation Piecing

A time-saving and more precise alternative for hand drawing a pattern onto tissue paper is photocopying the pattern onto a special tear-away paper used by quilters for foundation piecing. Several manufacturers produce this paper under different labels. Available through on-line sources and at some quilt stores, this paper is commonly referred to as paper for foundation piecing. Purchase a brand of paper in which the paper resembles newsprint. Do not purchase any brands in which the paper surface has a semi-gloss or is stiff to the touch. Load this paper into a photocopy machine as you would standard 8½" x 11" copy paper.

For an accurate photocopy of the pattern, make sure the pattern is flat against the copy machine glass. Cut off the excess paper from around the photocopy pattern leaving a ½" margin of paper. Using pins sparingly, pin in place on the fabric or art quilt.

When removing the paper pattern from the fabric, small paper fibers may remain on the right side of the fabric around the beads and thread. Use the point of a small scissor, a tweezers, or a pin point to coax the paper fibers off of the fabric.

Staggered Grid at 100% for Elevated Beading

Staggered Grid at 65% for Elevated Beading

Aligned Grid at 100% for Elevated Beading

Aligned Grid at 65% for Elevated Beading

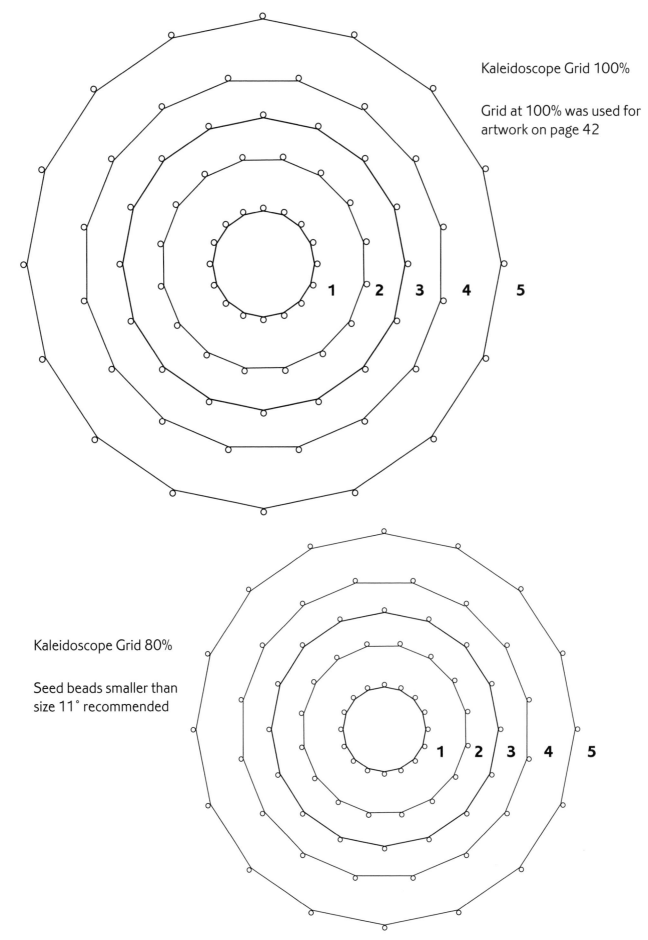

Kaleidoscope Grid 100%

Grid at 100% was used for artwork on page 42

1   2   3   4   5

Kaleidoscope Grid 80%

Seed beads smaller than size 11˚ recommended

1   2   3   4   5

Kaleidoscope Grid 120%

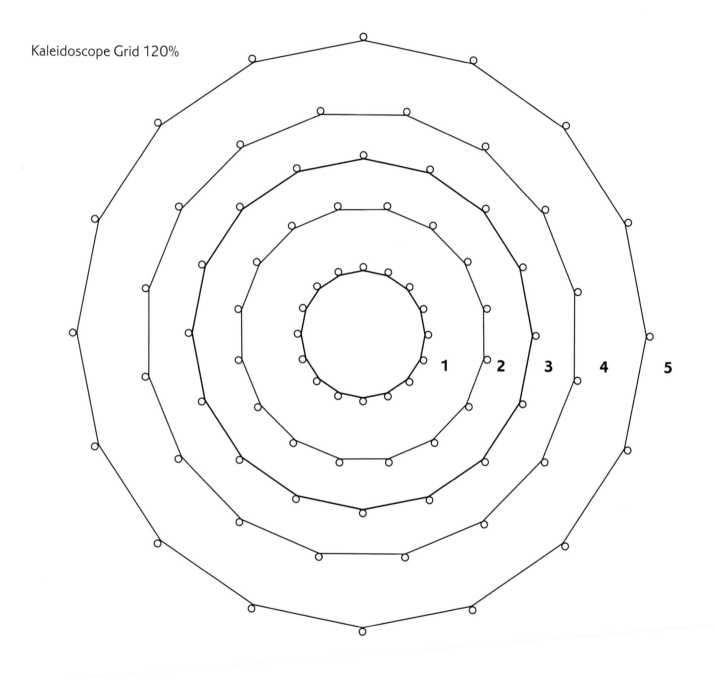

1   2   3   4   5

Patterns for Large Beaded Images

Dragonfly Wing Pattern

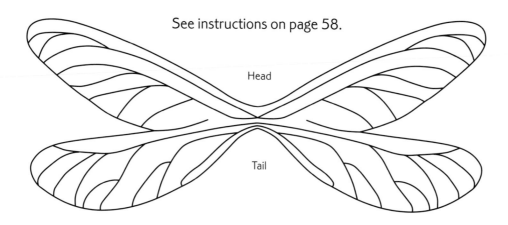

See instructions on page 58.

Head

Tail

Illustrations for Left-Handed Beaders

Beading illustrations which have a definite flow direction for right handed stitchers, are mirror imaged in this section for left-handed stitchers. The 🖐 inserted on the preceding pages indicates that an illustration for left-handed stitchers is included in this section.

For illustrations not include in this section, try turning the book upside down.

Basic Bead Embroidery and Beyond

Page 19, Illustration 1

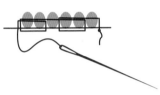

Page 19, Illustration 2

Page 20, Illustration 3A

3 2 1

Page 20, Illustration 3B

3 2 1 3 2 1

Beaded Kaleidoscope

Page 44, Illustration 2B

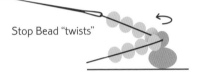

Stop Bead "twists"

Page 45, Illustration 3F

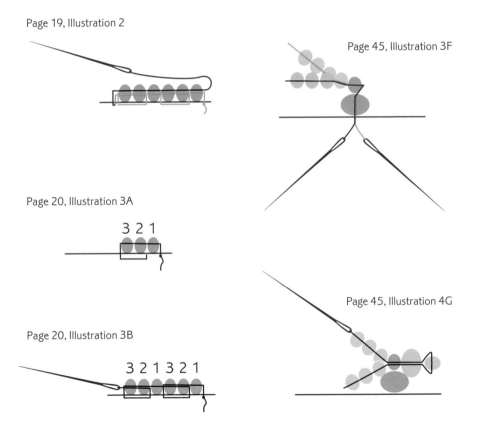

Page 45, Illustration 4G

Beaded Dragonfly

Page 62, Illustration 11

Page 45, Illustration 4H

Page 46, Illustration 7A

Left handed stitchers, work counter clockwise around Kaleidoscope patterns, pages 88–89.

Page 65, Illustration 17

Page 65, Illustration 18

Page 46, Illustration 7B

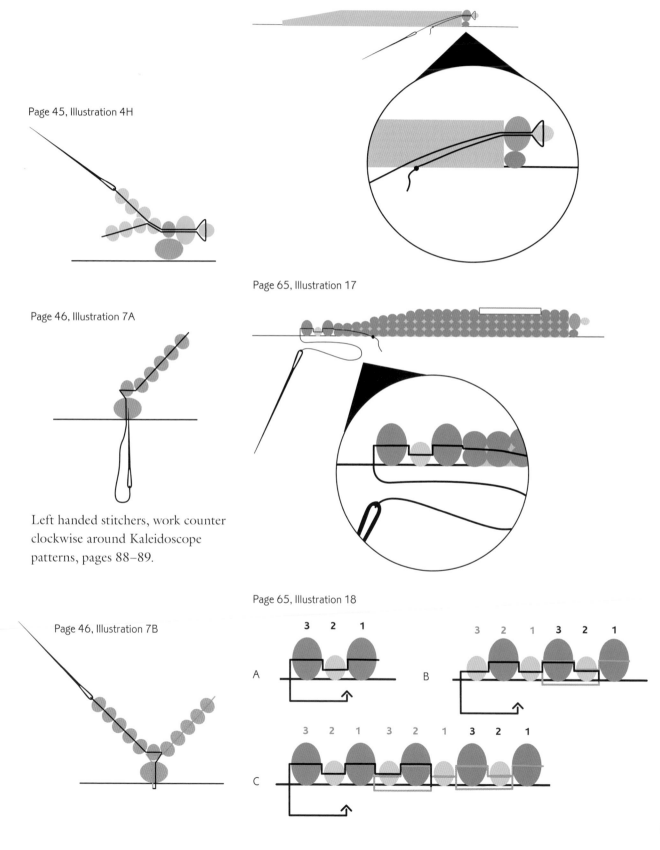

Beaded Snowflakes & Stars

Page 67, Illustration 2

Turn circle of 12 beads from Illustration 2 over in your hand as shown. Needle is exiting a lighter bead.

Left hand stitchers will be working clockwise.

Page 68, Illustration 3

Page 68, Illustration 4

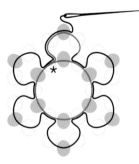

Page 68, Illustration 5

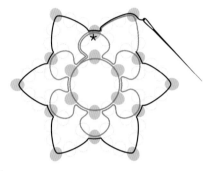

Page 68, Illustration 6

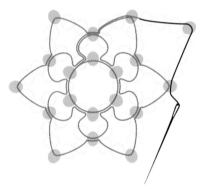

Page 68, Illustration 7

Page 68, Illustration 8

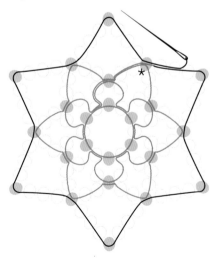

Page 69, Illustration 9A

Page 69, Illustration 9B

Page 69, Illustration 9C

Page 69, Illustration 9D

94

Glossary

Art quilt: Usually a fabric-based wall hanging to which any number of surface alterations or embellishments are applied

Asymmetrical: A design in which there is balance, but the elements are not duplicated on each side

Backing: The fabric layer on the back of the quilt

Baste: Long hand or machine thread stitches; can be permanent or removed when the step or project is completed

Batting: The layer between the quilt top and the back that provides the loft

Blocking: Steam or water mist applied to a quilt or quilt block while pinned firmly to a surface; when dry, the quilt or quilt block is returned to the original desired size and shape.

Bugle bead: A tubular glass bead

Darning foot: A special sewing machine foot used for free-motion stitching, circular with an open center

Facing a quilt: An easy method to add a quilt back and finish the raw edges of the quilt without adding binding

Finger press: Moving the index finger over an open seam while pressing downward on the seam with the finger

Fringe: A stack of beads that hang off the fabric surface

Paper for foundation piecing: A paper resembling newsprint, used by quilters for paper piecing

Quarter-inch presser foot: A special sewing machine foot used to sew quarter-inch seams for quilt construction

Quilt: Three fabric layers, top, batting, and back, with layers attached in some manner

Raw edges: The cut edges of a piece of fabric, cording, etc.

Right side of the fabric: The side of the fabric on which the beadwork is applied

Rotary cutter: A tool that looks like a pizza cutter and contains an extremely sharp blade capable of cutting through multiple layers of fabric. It must be used with a thick acrylic ruler and rotary cutting mat.

Rotary cutting mat: Used with the rotary cutter and rotary ruler, this mat protects your table surface during cutting.

Rotary ruler: Made of acrylic, these rulers partner with the rotary cutter to give clean, straight edges on multiple geometric shapes.

Saturation: Also referred to as color intensity. It is a color in its purest form; without white, gray, black or any other color added to it.

Seam allowance: The fabric between the seam stitches and the edge of the fabric

Seed beads: Small elliptical glass beads; the larger the number of the bead, the smaller the bead.

Shade: A color with black added to it

Sleeve: A fabric tube sewn horizontally on the top backside of a finished art quilt for hanging on a wall. A wooden slat with two drilled nail holes is inserted into the sleeve

Squaring up: The use of a square ruler on blocks or quilt tops to assure a right angle in all the corners

Stop bead: The top bead on a Stop Stitch. Named as such because it "stops the other bead(s) from falling off the fabric."

Stop stitch: Two beads stacked on to the fabric, the bottom bead laying on the fabric and the Stop Bead on top

Symmetry: A design in which one side exactly duplicates the other side as a mirror image

Tint: A color with white added to it

Thread tension: How tightly the thread is pulled when attaching a bead or making a thread stitch

Value: The degree of lightness or darkness of a color that is adjusted by adding black or white to the color

Wrong side of the fabric: The side of the fabric on which the thread knots and thread stitches are visible

Nancy Eha

was reportedly born with a needle in her hand. After exploring nearly every needle art, she began experimenting with beads after a chance encounter at her home state's number one tourist attraction, The Mall of America. Spending countless hours over many years asking creativity-stretching "what if?" questions of beads, she continues to develop new innovative beading techniques and create magical works of art.

As an internationally recognized artist, teacher, and author; Nancy shares her knowledge, passion, and pleasure for the subject of beading with others. She has written articles or has been featured in scores of magazines and books world-wide. Numerous awards for her ground-breaking beadwork and stellar teaching abilities include a grant from the Minnesota State Arts Board, and a teaching scholarship to attend the European Patchwork and Quilt Expo in Strasbourg, France.

In high demand as an instructor, Nancy makes learning fun, encourages confidence in students of all skill levels, and makes the seemingly complex easy to understand via small teachable steps. As she travels to present lectures and workshops, Nancy is inspired by those she meets and in continual awe of what can be created by hand and needle.

A life-long resident of Minnesota, Nancy currently resides in the scenic St. Croix River Valley near the historic town of Stillwater.

Visit Nancy's web site at: www.beadcreative.com